SERVING *the* GOOD *and the* GREAT

D09996171

THE AMAZING TRUE STORY OF
VIOLET LIDDLE

SERVING *the* GOOD
and the GREAT

VIOLET LIDDLE
As Told to Mary Batchelor

ZONDERVAN™

GRAND RAPIDS, MICHIGAN 49530 USA

ZONDERVAN™

Serving the Good and the Great
Copyright © 2004 by Mary Batchelor

Requests for information should be addressed to:
Zondervan, *Grand Rapids, Michigan 49530*

Library of Congress Cataloging-in-Publication Data

Liddle, Violet, 1922–
    Serving the good and the great : the amazing true story of Violet Liddle /
    Violet Liddle as told to Mary Batchelor.
       p. cm.
    ISBN 0-310-25395-0 (softcover)
    1. Liddle, Violet, 1922– 2. Women domestics—Great Britain—Biography.
    3. Baptists—Great Britain—Biography. 4. Number 10 Downing Street
    (London, England) 5. Great Britain—Biography. 6. World War, 1939-1945
    —Personal narratives, British. I. Batchelor, Mary. II. Title.
    CT788.L455A3 2004
    941.084'092—dc22

                                                          2004016140

Interior design by Beth Shagene

Printed in the United States of America

---

04 05 06 07 08 09 10 /❖ DC|/ 10 9 8 7 6 5 4 3 2 1

CONTENTS

INTRODUCTION

*I*t began when I read an article and interview in the London *Times* by Christina Hardyment, a journalist and social biographer. She told the story of Violet Liddle, a woman who had served as a housemaid for Bernard Shaw and his wife, and later waited at table for Prime Minister Winston Churchill and his family during World War II. I was fascinated by Violet's memories and intrigued by the comment that her ambition was not to be a parlour maid but a missionary.

A little detective work led me to Shaftesbury housing, where Violet had a flat, which was only ten miles from my home. By the time I met her, however, other writers and journalists were interested too, which makes me all the more grateful that Violet, on Christina's advice, chose me to write her story.

My literary agent and friend, Bill Neill-Hall, found me the ideal publisher in Zondervan, whose UK editor, Amy Boucher Pye, also lived a few miles away from me on a direct train link. She visited Violet with me and confirmed that Zondervan would publish our book in the US as well as the UK. When Amy took leave to have her first baby, one of her colleagues, Robert Hudson, a senior Zondervan editor in the US, took over the project and steered me through.

While Violet's own story is the main part of this book, I have written about other items of interest concerning the people she met and places she knew. These boxed annotations are not required reading – simply browse each topic as you encounter it and read the ones that interest you.

Sadly, during the period that Violet and I became friends, her sight began to fail. As the book was nearing completion, she heard the good news that room in a care home, near her brother and niece, had become vacant. Mere coincidence? Not in Violet's view.

Although she never fulfilled her ambition of becoming a missionary, her firm belief is that the story of her life will bring good news to many readers.

For my own part, knowing Violet has been an experience I wouldn't have missed. From her laughter, contentment and trust in God I have been helped on my own faith pilgrimage. I hope that her voice and character come alive through the story of her life and that others are entertained and also inspired by this amazing story of her brave and fulfilling life.

Mary Batchelor

ACKNOWLEDGEMENTS

I am most grateful to numberless people who so readily offered help on this project. The Society of Authors gave me advice and shared my enthusiasm at the outset when I needed it most. Welwyn Garden City and those at Tourist Centres gave help as did numerous people who not only helped with my research but did so with real kindness and interest. Stephen Bennett, then at Shaw's Corner, made us welcome and showed us round. My thanks to them all.

My warm thanks to Christina Hardyment for setting me on the way and to Violet's friends and relatives who helped me too.

My thanks to Amy Boucher Pye and to Robert Hudson of Zondervan for their wise editing and to Bill Neill-Hall for his calming support.

Above all my thanks to my family – to my husband, Alan, who has supported me unfailingly and taken over many duties to leave me free, and to our daughter, Pauline, and her husband Tony as well as our sons – Graham and his wife, Chriss, and Oliver and his wife, Jen. All have provided expert advice or loving care – or both.

David Saunders has been unfailing in giving much-needed assistance with computer and Internet worries and all our friends – especially our Church Home Group members – have shown interest throughout, never admitting to being bored by my enthusiasms, and above all supporting me with their prayers.

Mary Batchelor

SERVING *the* GOOD *and the* GREAT

PROLOGUE

I hear you have come from Chequers to help us.'

The voice was that of Winston Churchill – Prime Minister and hero of World War II – and he was addressing me.

I could scarcely believe it was really happening, but I managed to answer, 'Yes sir.'

There I was, summoned quite suddenly to Number 10 Downing Street, the official residence of the Prime Minister, at the very heart of London and at the height of the war. And I was to serve him lunch. . . .

I could never have imagined that such an experience was possible when I started out in service as a young and inexperienced fourteen-year-old. But what had promised to be a very ordinary life in domestic service brought me surprises and privileges, as well as hard work.

My life, in fact, has been filled with the wonderful and sometimes famous people I've been privileged to meet, along with the funny as well as the grim situations I've experienced both in wartime and in peace.

My name is Violet Liddle, and this is my story.

'I REMEMBER, I REMEMBER ...'

I was born Violet Elsie May Pond in 1922, four years after the end of World War I – the war to end all wars – and my brother, Clifford, was born two years later.

My earliest memories are of our home in Cambridge. While I was privileged to have been surrounded by the lovely buildings of that great university city, especially the famous chapel of King's College, our own home was not much more than a tenement.

KING'S COLLEGE CHAPEL

The famous Festival of Nine Lessons and Carols has been broadcast from King's College Cambridge every Christmas for over seventy years, even during World War II, when the precious stained-glass windows were removed for safe-keeping. The service begins at three o'clock on the afternoon of Christmas Eve. Although only college members and their guests have reserved seats, the radio carries the service worldwide. For all who hear it, the theme of the service is still, in the words of its founder Dean Milner-White 'the development of the loving purposes of God' seen 'through the windows and words of the Bible'.

What are my earliest memories? First, that it was a crime not to go to the toilet, which meant an outside one for us. Next, there was the old-fashioned mangle, which stood near the sink in the kitchen. People nowadays don't know what a mangle is, unless they've seen one in a museum, but there used to be one in every kitchen or wash-house before electric wringers were invented. The mangle was large – much taller than a child – and stood on heavy iron legs. It had an iron frame and two big wooden rollers, which were turned by a wooden handle attached to a large wheel. The housewife folded the wet clothes and then fed them in between the rollers and turned the handle. A bucket underneath caught the water that was squeezed out. For some reason I tried to move that mangle one day and poor little Clifford was in the way. His elbow was pinched. Though no real harm was done, it was a nasty moment for me – and for him.

Another vivid memory is of my mother standing on the stone steps that led up to the front door. She was dreadfully upset because Dad had fallen off

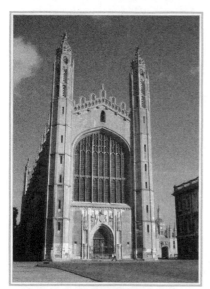

King's College Chapel at Cambridge

his bike. I think a dog had run across his path, and swerving to miss it, he had ridden off the road. Oddly, I have no memory of how badly Dad was hurt, just that dreadful moment of anxiety on the stone steps.

There was also some chinaware that we used at home that I specially loved. I used to lay the table, and Clifford and I had special plates with daisies round the edge. Many years later I saw a jam dish just like the one we had and felt a wave of homesickness for those faraway days.

For the first years of my life, my understanding of God was that he watched me continually and knew as soon I did anything wrong. That was because we had a framed Bible verse on the wall at home that read, 'Thou God seest me'. So I used to come down the stairs at a pretty fast pace, hoping that God wouldn't notice I was there.

Still, I don't really regret this introduction to God because it did instil in me an understanding that God is always around us, and I'm glad that over the years I've come to recognise that the verse is a promise of God's loving care and not a threat of punishment.

At some point, we moved to another home in Cambridge – one of some new houses that had been built, with fields all around and a little stream at the bottom of the lane. I fell into that stream on one never-to-be-forgotten day. I was leaning out to reach something, slipped and fell into the water. Clifford, who has always been my knight in shining armour, quickly pulled me out. Dripping wet, we dragged ourselves home, sure that we were in for a good telling-off from our parents. But we didn't get scolded at all. I realise now that our parents were only too thankful that we were safe and sound.

As a great treat I was allowed to take a neighbour's small child out in her push-chair, which I would push up and down the lane, picking the cowslips and violets and bluebells along the way and later putting them in jam-jars in the shed.

Sometimes on a Sunday afternoon my grandma – Mum's mother – would visit. I used to stand at the front gate, waiting for her, looking at all the different coloured pansies in bloom and gazing up the road for the first sign of Uncle Stan's car. He was married to Auntie Ethel, Mum's younger sister, who was only fourteen years older than me.

At last we'd spot the little Fiat car in the distance, Uncle at the wheel and Grandma in the back. They said she used to clutch at Uncle and tell him to sound his horn for safety's sake every time there was a turn in the road – all the way from London to Cambridge.

Uncle Stan was a clever man. He had invented a dimmer light switch, for instance, and sometimes he'd show us his designs. He was a good photographer too, and one day he set up his camera on a tripod to take a photo of me with my doll's pram and my precious doll inside it. He coloured his photos – an extra thrill in the days when photography was entirely black and white.

I suppose I was seven or eight when we moved again, this time to Saffron Walden. I really loved that house, which was old and stood next door to the church. Clifford used to complain that the bells kept him from concentrating, but I loved them, especially when they rang out for weddings on Saturdays and we could watch the bride coming out of church and see all the fine dresses of the wedding party.

We had a courtyard and no garden, but the public gardens were just opposite, and we could walk there as well as climbing the hill to watch the cricket matches in the field at the top. That hill! We had to climb it to get to school and then again on Sundays to go to chapel. Sundays always seemed to be cold and wet, and we'd arrive soaked and chilled to the bone.

SAFFRON WALDEN

Of all the spices in the world, the most precious is saffron. It is made from the threadlike stamens of the beautiful autumn crocus, every one hand-picked. Seventy-five thousand flowers are needed to make up one pound of saffron. It has been much sought after since medieval times in medicine, cooking and as a rich yellow dye. Merchants would come from all over England to buy saffron at Walden, and so it gained the name Saffron Walden. By the eighteenth century the trade had died out, and only the name remained in memory of its once famous trade.

Since I had always loved music, Dad arranged piano lessons for me while we were still back in Cambridge. When Miss Tucker, my teacher, came to the house, she would bring a bag of buns, which she munched while she taught me. She managed to teach me the basics, and I even won a couple of certificates. Being able to play has been useful at every stage of my life.

Lessons continued for a bit even after we moved to Saffron Walden, and when Dad was in

The ancient town of Saffron Walden

charge of the chapel service one year, my musical talent was
sometimes called upon. If there was no one else to play at a service, he would get me to do it, perched high on a stool. Since I
could only play three hymn tunes at that stage, which were
Rimington, Lloyd and *Crimond*, he used to choose hymns with
words to fit one of those three. I wonder if the congregation
noticed that we had the same few hymns every time I played.

Chapel was always an important part of family life – and
has remained so for Clifford and me to this day. Although we
were the only children belonging to the chapel and had to sit
as still as mice – and my hat pressed on my hair ribbon and
hurt my head – everyone was so kind and nice to us. I remember one lady, called Lilian Isaacson, who used to ask me for
Sunday dinner sometimes and that was a great treat. Looking
back, I realise that she was in service and could invite me when
her employers were out for the day.

STRICT AND PARTICULAR BAPTISTS

Violet and her family belonged to a branch of the Baptist church that was not part of the Baptist Union. The
word *Strict* stands for 'restricted' because membership
was 'restricted' to those baptised in one of the
churches. They were called *Particular* because they
believe that only those particular people chosen by God
can be saved. In the 1970s many of these churches com-
bined to form the Grace Baptist churches, which are
more open and outward-looking. They are committed
to Christian mission and have their own radio pro-
grammes. Violet belongs to one of these churches, and
her brother, Clifford Pond, is one of their pastors.

The Sunday School Anniversary was a red letter day. I wore my favourite dress, made of fine white cotton, with a three-tiered skirt. Then there was a splendid tea, laid out on boards balanced on top of the pews, to serve as tables. We had bread and butter and slices of cake – plain and fruit – and tea from a huge urn was carried in and set on the end of the board. Of course, there was also the ordeal of having to give recitations, but looking back, I'm glad of the training that gave us. We had to practise reciting our pieces beforehand and the super-intendent would sit in the very back row to make sure that he could hear every word distinctly.

WELWYN GARDEN CITY

Visionary entrepreneur Ebenezer Howard, born in 1850, dreamed of creating towns that were green and tree-filled, far from the smoke and dirt of big cities. Such towns would provide work, housing and everything needed for a pleasant, enjoyable life. Factories were to be situated just beyond the town. Good train and road systems would be provided, and electric power to take the place of coal and cut down on pollution. In 1903 his dream came true when he built the first Garden City in Britain, in Letchworth, Hertfordshire.

In April 1920, the second of his Garden Cities was begun near the village of Welwyn, where, in 1925, the imposing Shredded Wheat factory was built. Other industries soon followed. Newcomers were able to find work *and* accommodation for themselves and their families. Peartree School, where Violet was a pupil, opened in 1929.

The next major event in my life was *not* such a happy one.
We were uprooted from our Saffron Walden home and moved
to Welwyn Garden City. What a contrast! From the old and
beautiful to the new and ugly. WGC, as it was referred to, was
a new town, with houses built alongside new factories so as to
provide jobs and homes for lots more people. It was still under
construction when we arrived, and cement lorries constantly
rumbled up and down the road. I hated it all, but even then
I grasped the fact that Dad must have had problems with his
job and that we'd had to move so that he could get work. I've
learned since that he lost his previous job by being too hon-
est and hardworking. Some of the others were jealous and
wanted to get rid of him – and they succeeded.

One change for us when we moved to WGC was that Clifford and I were sent to the Open Baptist Church, a bit freer,
as you might guess, than the Strict and Particular Baptist
church that Dad belonged to. That was because there was no
Strict and Particular chapel near us. Mum went to the
Methodists, and it was just Clifford and I who walked to the
Open Baptist chapel each Sunday. At that time they did not
have a building of their own (they later had a proper building
put up, which is still there), so they used to meet in the Guide
hut. It got terribly hot in summer and cold in winter, but Clifford and I had happy times in that Guide hut. What I learned
there influenced the whole of the rest of my life. The people
were so kind to us, and it was when I was in that hut, in my
early teens, listening to a sermon, that I realised that Jesus was
calling me to follow him and I answered yes. I was the first
person to be baptised in that congregation.

One year I won a Sunday school prize there. It was called
Chopsticks, and it was all about missionary work in China. That
book started me on my life's ambition to be a missionary in

China. We were taught at Sunday school always to aim high. So although I never achieved my ambition to be a missionary, I believe that it's important at the time to strive for what you want to do. It may lead to some frustration, but that has to be corrected.

My first school was Peartree School. The headmistress was Miss Ling, a very imposing person. There were always pots of red geraniums on the polished red-tile windowsills in the corridor. From Peartree I went to Handside School, as it was called then. It was a good school with excellent teachers and very good discipline. One day two of the boys came into class looking what Miss Ward, the English teacher, considered 'unkempt'. Out they had to go and get washed and spruced up, and they wouldn't have dreamed of disobeying.

I liked school pretty well and wasn't bad at lessons. There were three streams, according to ability, and my problem was that I was put into the B stream first. Then they transferred me to the A stream, but I'd lost ground because the top stream had already begun French, and it was a job for me to catch up. But I was good at maths – at least all the time Mr Berry taught us. He was a funny little man, but I managed to do well until he left. But I just couldn't get on with his successor. I think I'm like that, a lot depends on how I get on with a person.

Of course there were the school holidays. Exploring the woods became so much more fun when Dad brought home a little puppy one November evening. What excitement! Dad got it so as to cure Clifford of his fear of dogs. We called her Flossie. One day we took her with us, along with a picnic of jam sandwiches and a basket for the blackberries we hoped to pick. I said, 'Stay,' while we searched for a good spot, but I didn't let her out of my sight while we were picking. She kept up with us bravely as we trudged back with a full basket, and it was only when we arrived home that she held up her paw, looking very pathetic. We found a thorn in it, yet she had never complained on the long walk home.

Sometimes we'd go into the town where one of the attractions was the Shredded Wheat factory. We were always hoping we'd be given free samples, but that didn't last long – they got used to seeing us there, so they sent us packing.

SHREDDED WHEAT

One day Henry D. Perky, a lawyer from Denver, Colorado, came across a man eating boiled wheat with cream to cure his indigestion. Perky saw a future in this remedy and invented a machine to press the grains together in strips. He baked the strips into biscuits, then toured the countryside in a horse-drawn wagon to sell his machines, taking sample biscuits to demonstrate the machine's virtues. But people wanted the biscuits, not the machines. So in 1893 Mr Perky opened a bakery, and the Shredded Wheat Company was born. Success followed quickly. By 1898 the biscuits were being imported to London. Soon Shredded Wheat became so popular that a British factory was needed, and the new town of Welwyn Garden City was the chosen site. In 1920 the first biscuit was produced in the brand new Shredded Wheat Factory. They are still made there today.

We didn't go away for a summer holiday as a family, but Mum and us children would go to stay for a fortnight with

Grandma, who lived in South London – in Stockwell, near Brixton. We'd either go by train or by Green Line bus (on which I was usually sick).

I can see Grandma now, standing by the stove and cooking the most delicious eggs and bacon that you've ever tasted. I picked

Shredded Wheat truck

up the fact that she had been in service before she was married, probably as a cook I guess.

Granddad worked in the Royal Mews, where the horses were kept. He could always tell us the best place to stand if we were going to watch special ceremonies like Trooping the Colour. But we never knew exactly what his job was. What a pity that people didn't talk about themselves and their work in those days! There's so much I'd love to know about them, but they didn't consider it was polite or proper to talk about themselves, and that's why I don't know any more about them.

I used to like to go shopping in Stockwell. You could buy a yard of material from the haberdasher's in Landor Road for fourpence three farthings in old money – that's 2p today. Then I'd buy broken biscuits cheap and deliciously sweet sticks of barley sugar. On one day of the holiday Auntie would take us both to Lyon's Corner House in London to have egg on chips. This was a real treat.

One day I plucked up courage and asked, 'Auntie, could I have an ice-cream?' I'd seen people at the next tables eating Neapolitan ice-creams (vanilla, strawberry and chocolate).

She said, 'Of course you can!' I've realised since that she must have spent all her week's money to treat us.

It was lovely being at Grandma's – there was no criticism or rebukes, and Auntie showed us such affection. I could live in the delightful world of my own imagining while Grandma and Mum chatted away non-stop, exchanging all the titbits of news. I would steal quietly away and make myself as nice as I could. I knew I was no beauty, but I could still make the best of myself. I went through to the scullery and had a thorough wash down, then plaited my hair carefully, put on my dress and carefully fastened the necklace I'd bought at Woolworth's. It was made of glass beads, alternate clear and blue and had cost sixpence. Then I went back to the grown-ups.

'Grandma, may I cook?' I'd wheedle, but there was never any problem. She'd give me a few pennies to buy one carrot, one turnip, one onion and two pennyworth of beef suet from the butcher's. I don't remember what meat I used. When I got back from the shops, I set out the pastry board, the rolling pin and all the other utensils I'd been taught to use at school. I never remember having any catastrophes, just a lovely sense of well-being about the whole thing. Even when I turned out her cupboards and put everything back *my* way, Grandma never complained.

On Sundays we went to Brixton Tabernacle, and Auntie and I used to link arms during the long sermon. I loved that and the feeling of friendship and affection that Auntie showed me. I think she wanted to make up for the love that was not openly shown to us at home. Sunday tea was special too, with tinned peaches and Libby's cream and golden syrup on our bread and butter. Looking back I realise that Grandma must have saved hard to afford all the extra expense of our stay with her. But I've never forgotten Grandma's patience and kindness, and many years later, when Grandma was dead, I told Auntie so. She was so pleased.

I haven't said very much about our Dad and Mum, but looking back, I realise that we didn't have a very comfortable home environment. Clifford and I never talked about it even to each other. Like most children, we took our family life for granted, that was the way things were. Before World War I Dad had been in the grocery trade, working for David Gregg's, a well-known grocery chain of businesses. Then he served in the war, and afterwards he couldn't get back into grocery as he wanted to. So he had a job as an insurance agent, going round on his bike to collect people's weekly premiums. He always had a pocket full of change so that no one could make the excuse of not paying up because they hadn't got the right money. But things were hard. When the electricity bill came in, Dad would say, 'We've got to cut back here.'

But there were good weeks, and then Dad would come home with fish and we'd have fish for tea on a Friday. Or else on a good week he'd bring a bag of toffees home on a Friday; he always carried the bag under his arm. We hadn't to say anything until we were given one. Of course we weren't given the bag, the toffees were doled out to us, and we had to wait. We were not encouraged to show excitement either. I think Dad was afraid that I'd turn out like Auntie, Mum's sister. She was bubbly and showed her feelings. I think I am a bit like her now, but it was a long time before I learned how to converse or have views of my own. We were encouraged to be seen and not heard, and when there were rules we were never given reasons for them.

Dad was away quite a bit, preaching at other chapels. Sometimes he'd be away for a night, and Mum would always cry when he went. I sat by her side, and she gave me her sewing-box to tidy. When Dad came back he always seemed to have caught a cold. I think he slept in damp, unaired beds where he was staying.

It was the strictness at home that made things hard for Clifford and me. After meals we weren't allowed to get up as soon as everyone had finished eating. We had to go on sitting at the table for a certain number of minutes, arms folded, completely still and silent. I would see Clifford's face twitching, as he did his best to make me giggle.

I believe in the Calvinist doctrines, but I do wish that Calvinism didn't so often produce hardness. I wish it could be more steeped in grace – grace shown to others based on God's wonderful love to us. All the hard rules about being separate should be tempered with love. I knew that if ever I brought a young man home he must believe in 'free grace, not free will'!

It wasn't the practice in those days for families to show their love in any way. I would never have run up to my parents and expect a hug, as children would today. I think it made it a bit difficult at first for us to show our feelings when we grew up, but there – we've not only survived, but we've so much to be thankful for. After all, that was our parents' way of bringing us up, and although it's their responsibility when you are young, later on you have to be responsible for yourself. You can't go on blaming your upbringing. And another thing – when I look back and think about it now, I can see that the early discipline stood me in good stead for all that the future had in store for me.

LEARNING THE HARD WAY

*A*t fourteen I knew exactly what I wanted to do with my life – I longed to be a missionary in China.

Of course, what I wanted to do didn't really count. That may sound strange to young people today, but in those days what mattered was what the teachers at school thought best and, more importantly, what my Dad decided I should do. Most of the teachers wanted me to go into Cresta Silks, which was one of the factories in Welwyn Garden City. Don't ask me what they thought I would do there because I've no idea, but they must have thought I was more suited to that than to domestic work. Dad thought otherwise. He had decided that I should go into domestic service, and it never occurred to me to rebel.

CRESTA SILKS

In 1925 Alec Walker persuaded an old friend, Tom Heron, to come down to the picturesque fishing village of Newlyn in Cornwall to help him at Chrysede, a new business he had set up, creating beautiful silks. Tom was a shrewd businessman but also a poet and member of the Christian Socialist Movement. Chrysede expanded, moved to St Ives and produced superb silks, which were sold to customers all over the world. In 1929, after disagreement among the directors, Tom moved his family to the new town – Welwyn Garden City – where he set up Cresta Silks, producing similar exclusive and unusual silk textiles and designs. His son, Patrick, who designed for the firm for a time, later became an internationally acclaimed artist. He returned to his childhood home in St Ives to join the group of artists there.

As you will have guessed by now, most children and young people in those days did what their parents wanted. I'm sure Dad wanted what was best for me because he was always good to me. I was never very strong, and he would bring home all sorts of remedies – like Scott's Emulsion – that he thought would do me good and build me up. I don't think he can have realised just how hard domestic work was. His idea was that I would learn all the things I needed to be able to do to prepare me for marriage. Perhaps it was because Mum hadn't been too good in that department that he wanted me to have a proper training.

GETTING EMPLOYMENT

By the end of the 1930s there were about one and a half million domestic servants in Britain, so there were plenty of employers wanting staff and 'domestics' needing jobs. As well as using the local Employment Exchange, those looking for staff consulted the specialist employment agencies that had sprung up. One woman, Lily Margate, a housemaid looking for a job, described her first visit to the Mayfair Agency in London. She was not sure which of the two entrances to use: 'When I stepped inside the elegance of white and gold paint, velvet curtains and delicate chairs and sofas piled with cushions I just stood on the thick carpet and stared until a very smart woman came sailing towards me. She knew at once . . . "Please go next door, this is for ladies only" and she gave me a hard poke in the back towards the door . . . I went to the next door which said, "Please walk in". My word, what a different scene this was. No thick carpet here, or velvet curtains, no fragile chairs or cushions. The floor was covered with brown linoleum, benches lined each side of the room, one side for maids, the other for menservants; down one length of the room were small desks with chairs each side for interviews. I sat down to await my turn and eyed the young men on the opposite bench.' (From *Life Below Stairs in the Twentieth Century*, by Pamela Horn)

As far as I know my first job was fixed through an arrangement between the employment agencies and my school. I was to work as between-maid with a Mr and Mrs Holdsworth, who lived on the edge of the Hatfield Estate, in a house that had once been a farmhouse and was now rented out to gentry. Mr Holdsworth was an employee of the Victoria Wine Company.

THE VICTORIA WINE COMPANY

William Hughes, a gentleman with very definite ideas, opened his first shop in London in 1865 and named it after Queen Victoria. He sold wine to ordinary people (who usually drank beer or gin) in pleasant surroundings. When Hughes died twenty-one years later, at the age of fifty, he owned ninety-eight shops. He employed women not only to serve but to manage as well, an unheard of innovation. As well as being good business-women, they must also have ladylike manners, dress in black and wear their hair in a bun, in the style of Queen Victoria. Hughes wanted to show the world that women could succeed in management as well as men.

I suppose they were gentry. Mrs Holdsworth certainly dressed for dinner every evening. I can picture her now in the voile dresses she usually wore. They had a small loop of cotton sewn to the hem so that she could put her little finger through the loop and hold the skirt clear of the ground as she walked. That way she wouldn't trip over it or get the hem dirty.

FASHION IN THE THIRTIES

Wearing the right clothes at the right time was extremely important in the 1930s, especially for women. Ladies like Mrs Holdsworth would have changed three times a day, selecting dresses suitable for morning, afternoon and evening. New pastimes, like motoring in open-topped cars, created a market for special outfits. Hollywood also made a huge impact on fashion, and in Britain, royalty had a great influence as well. In 1934 Princess Marina of Greece married the Duke of Kent, the youngest son of King George V and Queen Mary. Tall, beautiful and elegant, she captured the public imagination, and when she was photographed wearing a coat of a greenish-blue shade, that particular colour soon became a fashion 'must' and has since been known as 'Marina green'.

I lived in, but went home on my bicycle on my day off. I wasn't exactly well-off with the wage I earned, and I was also paying my parents back for my bike as well as my morning uniform, which they had bought for me. In those days, maids were expected to provide their own morning uniforms. My dress was a pale bluish-grey colour and had a good big apron. When doing dirty jobs, I had a rough apron to put on top of that. Employers were responsible for providing the afternoon uniform, which, at the Holdsworths', was a black alpaca dress with a white collar, which was attached with a press-stud at the neck. There was a little white apron and cap and white cuffs that came off for washing – quite smart and trim.

Fashion picture from 1930s

At that stage I only possessed two pairs of shoes, one for going out and one pair for indoors, and I'm ashamed to say that the indoor ones had holes in them. I lined them with cardboard because I just couldn't afford another pair. But I did treat myself to one pretty set of underwear. I can remember going into the shop in Welwyn Garden City and choosing pink Celanese. I treated it with great care, keeping it wrapped in tissue paper and only wearing it on my afternoon off.

In large households, the housekeeper was in charge of the staff, but in smaller ones, like the Holdsworths', the cook gave orders. It seemed to be the fashion at that time to engage temporary cooks, so you can imagine that there was a good bit of chopping and changing even during my time there. I can remember one whose stay was extra short. She was German, and at one meal she served up mince wrapped in cabbage leaves. Mr Holdsworth did not consider this proper food and marched down to the kitchen himself and sent her packing.

I got on with most of the cooks fairly well, and we always had good food. Some of them used to bring back to the kitchen any food left over from dinner in the dining-room, then put it on one big dish for us to help ourselves for our supper. When I've talked to other girls who have been in domestic work they have said how mean their people were about food. I certainly didn't have that problem in either of the jobs I had.

In addition to the cook, there was Olive, the housemaid, and Amy, the parlour maid. As a between-maid, I wasn't allowed to serve in the dining-room. My job was to wait on the rest of the staff and fetch anything they wanted at our meals in the kitchen. I don't want to be unkind, but I can't honestly say that they were a good bunch. Amy was the best, but I didn't have much to do with her, except when Cook had time off and she and I were left in charge. Amy used to give us a little treat on those days. Cook made coffee-walnut sponge cake for the dining-room but rock cakes for the kitchen. When she wasn't about, Amy would pop the rock cakes in the oven to warm them up. They went down a lot better that way. But if Cook had found out what she'd been up to, she would have been in hot water.

ROCK CAKES

Rock cakes – or buns – were extremely plain and inclined to be dry and hard. Here's a recipe from an English cookbook of the mid-1940s. Ingredients: -1/2 lb. (225g) Flour; -1/2 teaspoon Baking Powder; 1 -1/2 oz (50g) Butter; 1 -1/2 oz (50g) Sugar; 2 oz (60g) Currants or Sultanas; 1 Egg; a little Milk. Work the butter into the flour then add the dry ingredients. Mix into a stiff dough with the beaten egg and milk. Put spoonfuls on a greased baking sheet and bake in a fairly hot oven for about 15 minutes.

I soon discovered that there was a right and a wrong way for doing everything, and these rules were pretty much the same whatever household you were in. Olive, the housemaid, had to teach me how to do the bedrooms. There were slops to empty – everyone used a chamber pot at nights then – and the beds to be made. They had to be done just so, the pillows arranged with the fancy bits outside and the blankets covered over with muslin. After that the rooms had to be cleaned.

I felt really pleased one day when one of the guests paid me a compliment. She saw me cleaning the bedroom door,

Violet in maid's uniform

dusting and polishing all the folds and crevices in the woodwork. (There were plenty of those in Victorian doors.) She stopped and said, 'That's marvellous; that's quite the right way to do it.'

Doing the work the right way was important in the kitchen too. When I first went there I was told to scrub the kitchen table. I did it the way I'd been taught at school and very nearly lost my job. I'd done it the wrong way. At school we'd learned to scrub the table in sections but that means that you end up with ridges of scum all the way across. So I learned pretty quick to do it the proper way, from one end to the other. Most of the kitchen work was hard slog, and to add to that we hadn't got all the cleaning aids we can get today. The only way of getting rid of grease was by using soda crystals in the water, so in went a handful of soda to all the washing-up water and the water in the bucket for scrubbing too. It ruined my hands and I used to say that I would never get a boyfriend with hands so rough and red from the soda.

Scrubbing the kitchen floor was one of the worst jobs. I had to get down on my hands and knees, and scrub hard at the tiles. As well as soda, we had a little square mesh container with a handle. The soap was put in the mesh basket, and then we swished it around in the hot water. Not that there was an endless supply of hot water either. We had to eke it out so that there would be plenty for the people in the front of the house and their visitors. Not only did I have to clean the kitchen floor, but the walk-in larder that opened off the kitchen. There was a dividing ridge of wood across the doorway, and that, to me, marked the limit of how far I had to go. But not to Cook. I would scrub the kitchen floor and stop exhausted at the larder door. Cook's bedroom led off the kitchen, and I'm sure she would lie in wait for me because she would suddenly appear as if by magic and shout out, 'Open the larder door and do that bit of floor too!' And even though I was aching and hurting all over, I had to do as I was told and get on with it.

The boiler, which was like a closed-up stove, had to be stoked with coke. 'Coke' didn't mean then what it does today. It was a kind of dull-looking fuel – coal that had been treated so that it didn't burn so fast or bright. The boiler had to be raked through and the ash-pan emptied. Then I had to use the tongs to take out all the waste bits of clinker that wouldn't burn. Next I had to clean the kitchen range. That was fired by solid fuel too. Later on we had an oil-fired stove, but I don't remember that it was much of a success. The stove and outside of the ovens had to be black-leaded and the steel rods polished with *Zebo*.

Were there any good times? Once we had a good laugh when a Dr Lamb came to lunch. When she let him in, Amy, the parlour maid, was sure that she'd get it all wrong – and sure enough she did. She came bursting back into the kitchen with her cheeks burning. 'I *did* do it wrong!' she wailed, 'I said, "Dr Lunch, the lamb is ready"!'

But no, we didn't have a lot of fun, but it was good grounding and prepared me for my next job. As soon as my eighteen months were up, I was due for promotion – and that meant moving on.

SHAW'S CORNER

I had not given up my ambition to be a missionary in China. Since nursing seemed to be the best qualification for missionary work, I went to see the teacher at my old school and asked her whether it was possible for me to train as a nurse. I was fifteen or sixteen at the time. She suggested St Mary's Hospital in Paddington, but a London hospital like that seemed a bit above me. Unfortunately, nothing came of it, and later on, when I was in the Army, I again tried to get into nursing, but at that point they told me that they had enough nurses.

After eighteen months with Mr and Mrs Holdsworth, as I said, it was time to move on – especially if I was expecting to get promotion. I was told that I would have an interview for a job as housemaid with a Mr and Mrs Shaw at Ayot St Lawrence, a small village in Hertfordshire, not far from Welwyn. I'm really not sure how the interview came about, but I was told that the cook-housekeeper, Mrs Higgs, was going to come across to our house to interview me. It was impressed upon me that I was to call her 'Madam' if I wanted to get the job. She rolled up in style, driven by Mr Shaw's chauffeur, but I didn't call her madam. So after she'd gone, there were long faces and the comment, 'You won't get the job.' But I did.

George Bernard Shaw

I'm not so sure that it *was* in order to call her 'Madam' when she was one of the staff herself.

That is how I came to work at the home of the famous playwright George Bernard Shaw.

Working for such a famous person may sound exciting and important, but to tell you the truth, I hadn't even heard of him at the time. He was well known in literary circles, of course, but not among folk like us. I found out later about some of his other exploits when he was younger. He used to write pamphlets for causes he felt strongly about, to tell the public about some of the wrongs in society. He helped the Salvation Army over the matter of child prostitution. William Booth wanted to stop the trade in young girls that was going on in England, and Mr Shaw supported him. But the government didn't really want to do anything about it. He campaigned for lavatories for women in London and horse troughs in the streets for the thirsty horses. That was before there were cars and vans, of course.

GEORGE BERNARD SHAW – AS OTHERS SAW HIM

Shaw was not considered handsome. One lady, who was very much in love with him, even admitted that he was 'very plain'. Others were more outspoken. Wilfred Blunt, the poet, described him as 'an ugly fellow . . . his face a pasty white, with a red nose and a rusty red beard, and little slatey blue eyes. Shaw's appearance, however, matters little when he begins to talk, if he can ever be said to begin, for he talks always, in his fine Irish brogue.' But looks weren't everything. Edith Bland (the English children's writer E. Nesbit) wrote: 'He has a fund of dry Irish humour that is simply irresistible. He is the grossest flatterer of men, women and children impartially I ever met, and is horribly untrustworthy as he repeats everything he hears and does not always stick to the truth.'

MRS CHARLOTTE SHAW
(CHARLOTTE PAYNE-TOWNSEND)

'I had a perfectly hellish childhood and youth,' Mrs Shaw once declared. She was born in Cork, Ireland, in 1857, into an upper-class family. Her father was a gentle-natured man who was utterly at the mercy of his domineering wife, Charlotte's mother. 'It was a terrible home,' Charlotte observed, her mother 'could not bear opposition; if it was offered she either became quite violent or she cried. She constantly cried. She felt (genuinely felt) she had sacrificed her life for us and my father (we were two, my sister and myself) and she never ceased telling us so.' Charlotte was sure that her mother was responsible for her father's early death.

Once she was a widow, Mrs Payne-Townsend's aim was to marry off her two daughters as successfully as she could – into the aristocracy if possible. But Charlotte was not prepared to go the way of her father and be manipulated and dominated as he had been, so she made up her mind that she would not get married at all. Mother and daughters set off on a tour of Europe where Charlotte refused every offer of marriage she received. When she was thirty-four, her mother died, leaving Charlotte free at last.

In 1895 Beatrice Webb described Charlotte as 'a large, graceful woman with masses of chocolate brown hair. She dresses well, in flowing white evening robes she approaches beauty. At moments she is plain. By temperament she is an anarchist, feeling any regulation or rule intolerable, a tendency that has been exaggerated by her irresponsible wealth. . . . She is fond of men but impatient of most women . . . sweet-tempered, sympathetic, genuinely anxious to increase the world's enjoyment and diminish the world's pain.'

A year later Charlotte met Bernard Shaw, and in the summer of 1896 they were both guests at the Webbs' summer house-party where they talked, walked and cycled together. The friendship grew, and Charlotte soon began to help Shaw as his unpaid secretary.

I was barely sixteen when I started work with Mr and Mrs Shaw. People are curious to know how much I earned. I was paid £1 7s 6d a month – that's one pound thirty-seven and a half pence in today's money. When I was given a rise of 6d (two and a half pence), I was expected to thank Mrs Shaw profusely and show my gratitude by doing my work even better. But of course money went much further then, and we had our board provided.

Mr and Mrs Higgs had been with Mr and Mrs Shaw when they lived in London and then came to Ayot when the Shaws bought the house there. Mr Higgs did the garden with the help of Fred Drury, the under-gardener, and Mrs Higgs was in charge indoors as cook-housekeeper. I owe a lot to her for the training she gave me. There was also Maggie, the parlour maid, who was Irish and a bit older than I was, and Mr Day, the chauffeur, who would sometimes lend a hand in the garden, but in a rather superior way, because of his regular situation. When it rained, Mr Higgs would get Fred to make good use of his time by cleaning our bikes. Fred never minded, and Maggie and I were only too pleased.

SHAW AND CHARLOTTE'S MARRIAGE

Shaw found Charlotte an enormous help with his work. She could decipher his shorthand and sometimes took down his articles from dictation; she typed out the manuscripts of his plays and prepared them for the publishers. But Charlotte still wanted to be in control of her own life and would take off on a trip abroad at a moment's notice. Shaw was dismayed; a substitute secretary just didn't fill her place.

Charlotte, like Shaw, had decided never to get married, but she began to think that she *would* like to take their friendship further and actually suggested to Shaw that they should get married. When Shaw refused, partly because she was rich and he was poor, Charlotte packed her bags and went abroad, refusing all Shaw's pleas to come back.

Shaw went to pieces. He had injured his foot; it became infected, and an abscess formed. He bombarded Charlotte with pitiful letters, and at last she returned. She found him in a dreadful state of muddle and mess, sitting in his flat amid scattered papers and half-eaten bowls of porridge, so she carried him off to her own flat and looked after him.

By this time Shaw had made some money from his play *The Devil's Disciple* and felt more on equal terms with Charlotte. So on 1 June 1898 they were married. Shaw was still on crutches and arrived at the Register Office wearing an old patched jacket, badly frayed. He told the tale afterwards that he had been mistaken by the registrar for 'the inevitable beggar who completes all wedding processions'. He insisted that the registrar nearly married the bride to his friend Wallas, one of the witnesses, who was tall and imposing.

Only a week before the wedding Shaw had insisted that if he should marry it must be kept secret, but he himself wrote the report that appeared in *The Star* on 2 June. It read: 'As a lady and gentleman were out driving in Henrietta Street, Covent Garden, yesterday, a heavy shower drove them to take shelter in the office of the Superintendent Registrar there, and in the confusion of the moment he married them. The lady was an Irish lady named Miss Payne-Townsend and the gentleman was George Bernard Shaw.'

Ayot was a 'weekend house' at that time, because Mr and Mrs Shaw lived in London during the week, at their flat in

Whitehall Court. They came down to Ayot for the weekends. Quite often Mr Day would drive up to London on a Friday just to collect their luggage, and they would travel by train, which they liked doing. Then they would be off to London again on Monday morning.

FRED DAY

In 1919 Shaw had complained in a letter that 'travelling is still very troublesome', and that same year Mrs Shaw engaged Fred Day as chauffeur. He was to stay with them for thirty-one years. When they drove out in the car Shaw sat beside Fred in the front with Mrs Shaw in the back, on a seat specially upholstered and draught-proofed for her. Mr Shaw would take the wheel before lunch, driving very slowly when Mrs Shaw was present and very fast when she was not. Fred observed that Mr Shaw's chief error was to mistake the accelerator for the brake. The local dogs came to know him well and would crawl under the car and play dead until Mr Shaw crawled in after them, when they would leap out barking.

Fred Day, like every good servant, kept family life strictly apart from work. One day, during a downpour of rain, Mr Shaw noticed that Fred gave a small wave to a woman and child who were waiting, drenched, at the bus-stop. He asked who they were and Fred admitted shamefacedly that they were his wife and child. 'Stop!' Shaw shouted, 'turn the car round, we must take them home.' At the bus-stop he got out of the car, put his arm round Mrs Day's shoulder and helped her into the car, where she sat frozen with nervousness and embarrassment. Such behaviour towards staff was unheard of. Later on Mr Shaw offered to pay for Fred's daughter to train as a schoolteacher. Fred was staunchly loyal and confessed that he would 'do anything for Mr Shaw'.

When Mr and Mrs Shaw had left for the week, we still kept busy with a regular routine of work. My first job was to take the flowers out of all the rooms and put them in the pantry. I always rescued the ones that weren't dead – I couldn't bear to see them thrown out – and Mr Higgs approved of that. (I still retrieve flower heads that have been knocked off when I see them on the floor in the florist's.)

Mrs Shaw loved flowers – foxgloves and scabious and flowers like that – and she liked to have bowls of polyanthus on the windowsills arranged in old-fashioned vegetable dishes

Henry Higgs

with a glass rose to hold the flowers firm. Every year when the wild roses came out in the hedgerows, Mrs Higgs would pick a bunch specially for Mrs Shaw. When Mr Maisky (he was the Russian ambassador) came to visit, he almost always brought Mrs Shaw a potted azalea, with a pink bow tied around it, and that would be put on the stand in the hall.

Mr Shaw didn't approve of picking flowers, and there were

never any in his study or in the
dining-room. It wasn't that he
wasn't fond of flowers, but I'm
told he used to say, 'You like
children, but that doesn't mean
that you cut off their heads and
put them in water.'

The next job for Maggie and
me on a Monday morning would
be to get on with the bedrooms.
That was long before the days of
central heating, so there were
open fires in all the rooms and
they had to be cleared. The beds

Clara Higgs

were stripped and remade. Mr Shaw's bed was on rollers
attached to the floor, so that we could pull out the bed and do
the other side thoroughly. Then the rooms had to be cleaned.
There were no wall-to-wall carpets in those days, so the
wooden floor surrounds had to be polished on hands and
knees. Maggie did all the windows – I can see her now, polishing the brass arms that opened and shut them. The brass
has been blacked over now, I'm sorry to say. I suppose it saves
work, but it spoils the look of them.

When the war came in 1939, Mr and Mrs Shaw spent
more and more time at Ayot. Since I had reached the age of
eighteen, I was due to be called up into the Services, but
because Mr and Mrs Shaw were elderly and needed looking
after, I could apply for my call-up to be deferred. Mrs Higgs
and I had to go to Queen's Gate in London to plead our
cause, and I was 'reserved' or exempt from going into the Services, at least for a time.

CALL UP TIME

Although Neville Chamberlain, British Prime Minister, had announced 'Peace in our time' when he alighted from his plane in 1938, many people realised that war with Germany was still likely. Many men left their jobs and volunteered in the National Services. But the government needed skilled people to remain in their jobs, so a list of 'reserved' occupations was drawn up. The day that war was declared against Germany, 3 September 1939, men between the ages of eighteen and forty-one were called up into the armed forces, later extended to fifty-one.

In 1941, for the first time, women were called up. This rule applied to all unmarried women aged eighteen to thirty. Those in work of national importance were 'reserved' and others were directed to munitions factories or could apply to be 'land girls', helping farmers in the vital work of growing food. Boards were set up locally to deal with over five million applications that employers made to have their workers' call-up 'deferred'. Mrs Higgs went before one of these boards with Violet to apply for her to stay at Ayot.

When the London bombing began, the Shaws came to live full-time at Ayot so our routine changed. My day began at 6.30 a.m. I'd come downstairs and always find Maggie had got there first. She loved her cup of tea so there would be a pot brewing, and someone, I never knew who, used to prepare a piece of bread and butter for each of us and cover it over for the night. I can tell you that slice of bread and butter tasted really good! Not all staff were treated so well. Most had to wait till about eight o'clock – after they'd done lots of hard jobs – before they had a bite to eat. And they were young, growing girls. So we were very fortunate.

Open fires provided the warmth in the downstairs rooms too, and that made for an awful lot of dirt and hard work. We prepared everything the night before, getting the materials ready to light the fires next morning. First I'd lay a bundle of twigs on a sheet of newspaper. The London *Times* was best because the sheets were biggest. I'd fold the paper over into a kind of envelope, then stack up three or four of these bundles in a row by the pantry door.

Next morning I'd collect my housemaid's box with all my tools, put a rough cloth on the hearth and begin. First of all, the fires from the day before had to be cleared. Any unburned coals – and they were still hot – had to be removed before we lifted out the grating that fitted over the well of the fire. There was a special tool to hook between the slats so the grating could be picked up and lowered gently on to the hearth. Then the ash in the well beneath had to be cleared out with a special scoop. The grating was hot and really heavy – maybe it wasn't all that heavy, but it seemed so then – but it *must not* be dropped on the hearth because the clatter would disturb Mrs Shaw upstairs in bed – and then there would be trouble. I can tell you those hot coals and the hot ash between them played havoc with my hands. When I visit Ayot now, the fires look so small, but at the time they didn't, and clearing and lighting them seemed an exhausting job. I suppose it *was* hard work for someone young and not very robust.

After we'd done the fires, Maggie cleaned the dining-room, and I did the drawing-room, study and hallway and of

Shaw's house in a photo taken by Shaw himself

course the stairs. Those stairs! I've dreamed about them many times since. There were two flights to be cleaned, and they had to be done before Mrs Shaw was up. The front stairs, kept for Mr and Mrs Shaw and visitors, were carpeted, with a white surround and skirting board, brass stair rods and a polished banister. Once the stair carpet had been cleaned – with dustpan and stiff hand-brush on each step – the skirting had to be restored to whiteness and the banister polished. Every stair rod had to be removed, polished with brass cleaner and put back in its place. And all this had to be done in silence, so that Mrs Shaw wouldn't hear in the bedroom upstairs.

But it was the back stairs, not the front ones, that were the real nightmare. There were four flights of them, all covered in linoleum, and washing them was exhausting. I was only sixteen when I'd started at Ayot and small for my age, and I hadn't very much strength or staying power. It was a drain on the energy level, as I would put it, but no one considered such weakness in young girls in those days. Sometimes I didn't know how I'd get the next stair done, but I'd pray there on my knees, and somehow I'd have the strength to carry on and finish the lot.

My next job was to take Mrs Shaw her morning tea. As I put my hand on the bedroom door handle I would send up a quick prayer that I would do everything to her satisfaction. It was important not to ruffle anything or make a sound, and I was so afraid of doing something wrong. It was as if you had to be there and yet *not* be there. There was a proper order for doing everything and a proper way to do it. First I had to plump up the pillows for her. Even one tiny pillow she had, that was the softest of soft, still seemed to hurt her. Then there was a whole regiment of things that I had to put on her side table – eye-shades and all kinds of things like that, and I had to remember them all.

After that, I prepared Mrs Shaw's bath. It was about a foot high, made of reinforced papier-mâché, and it was kept under her bed. I had to drag it out – very quietly – and put it on a blanket that I had spread ready on the floor in front of the fire. I arranged her three towels (for face, hands and bath) on the stand – soft, medium and hard, in that order, with the monogram facing the front. Then I carried jugs of hot water upstairs from the kitchen. I never knew Mrs Shaw to use the toilet on that landing, so there were slop-pails to fetch and carry and her commode to be seen to as well. All this while Mrs Shaw was still in bed, and I was trying hard not to be clumsy or make a sound. You can understand why I needed to offer that swift prayer for patience and skill each morning. And the Lord *did* help me because I never remember any complaints.

We had to watch discreetly for Mrs Shaw to come down-stairs, and then Mrs Higgs usually helped me to tip the water from the bath into a pail. Then I'd empty the commode – I never thought anything of it. Mrs Higgs helped me make the beds. Then there was the cleaning to be done.

I think I had only one breakage in all the time I was there. Mrs Higgs and I were doing the hall – we had been spring-cleaning. Something fell onto the piano and broke. I thought Mrs Higgs was responsible, but she blamed me, so we begged to differ.

Just before lunch we'd scoot upstairs and change into our black-and-white uniforms. After lunch had been served and cleared up and the staff had eaten their meal in the kitchen, there were plenty of other jobs to do. We weren't given any time off in the day. When it was the right season there was fruit to be prepared for bottling and making jam, and failing that, there was always mending to be done.

The sheets had to be turned sides to middle, to make them last longer. You see the middle of the sheets wore out first, but the sides that were tucked in still had good wear in them. So the unworn parts had to be at the centre and the middle sewn to the sides. We didn't have a sewing machine, so all that stitching and hemming had to be done by hand. Can you imagine how long that took? There was a so-called staff-room upstairs but we never used it. The house was always cold so we did everything in the kitchen where the range kept it warm and cosy.

Towards the end of my time there we used to sit for hours mending the curtains and bedspreads. The backing on them was wearing thin so we cut the embroidery off and appliquéd it onto fresh backing. They were beautiful curtains with a pattern of branches with little birds and different flowers on them. I think they were made by the William Morris firm because I know Mrs Shaw favoured his designs. But they aren't at Shaw's Corner now – I was told that the mites got at them in the end.

WILLIAM MORRIS (1834–96)

'Have nothing in your houses which you do not know to be useful or believe to be beautiful' – that was the advice of William Morris, poet, printer, painter, and designer, in 1880, and he was the one man above all others to make that possible. As well as a love for beauty, he had a sharp eye for the practical and useful. He hated the ugly, mass-produced Victorian furniture and house design that he saw around him and dreamed of communities like the medieval guilds where crafts-people could work together to create beautiful and useful objects.

Morris also designed tapestries, furniture and textiles. When Morris and Company opened a shop in London's fashionable Oxford Street to sell his hand-woven tapestries, orders flooded in, including one from Queen Victoria for St James's Palace and later for her new mansion at Balmoral. In 1862 Morris began to design wallpaper, the thing he's best remembered for. In the twenty-first century his wallpapers are just as beautiful and nearly as popular as they were in the nineteenth.

Spring-cleaning was an annual ritual. There were coal fires in all the rooms and no vacuum cleaners, so by the time the spring arrived, the house was sadly in need of a good clean through.

The chimney-sweep would be booked to clear out all the winter's soot from the chimneys, and then cleaning began in earnest. This is the way we did it at Ayot.

If there were flowers in the room, they'd be removed and taken to the pantry, then we'd take the ornaments out and put them in a secure place. All the furniture that could be moved was put in the centre of the room and covered with dust sheets, which were neatly mitred and pinned to secure them. The curtains would be shaken but not very often cleaned. Then the fireplace had to be cleaned and the copper coal scuttle polished. We'd lay the fire with paper and sticks and put white paper in front behind the bars. The walls and high pictures were reached with a long cobweb brush and after that we cleaned the carpets. Next we did windows and the white skirting board, polished the wood surround to the carpet before polishing first the large then the small pieces of furniture. Then at last we'd be ready to arrange the room the right way again and put all the ornaments back in place.

In the evenings, even though we had finished work for the day, we were still on the premises and still on call. If they wanted us for anything we would always go – and willingly. After all, that was what we were there for, and it seemed more like a privilege than a duty, it somehow justified our existence.

I have only one regret about my time at Ayot, and that was the fact that Mrs Higgs never gave me the opportunity to do any actual cooking. (I think she did once let me make pastry, but she complained that I was too heavy-handed.) Perhaps that's why I've never been endeared to cooking. But the fact of the matter was that Mrs Higgs couldn't afford for anything to go wrong – she dare not risk her reputation. She was a marvellous cook, and I never heard any complaints about the food. We had the same food in the kitchen that they had in the dining-room, and that's more than can be said for many households. The people in the village reckoned that ours was the best household to be in. In other places they would count out even the number of potatoes that the staff were allowed. But we ate well.

Mr Shaw was a convinced vegetarian, but Mrs Shaw liked meat – so there was plenty to be prepared in the kitchen. My main job was doing the vegetables. Mr Higgs would bring them straight from the garden into the scullery, where I'd wash them thoroughly in the sink. Then I'd go to my place at the wooden kitchen table (I've scrubbed that a good few times!) and cut, slice and chop according to what was needed. They had a large hors-d'oeuvre dish, and we used to put aspic jelly in the middle and arrange the vegetables all around. The beetroot was diced, the celery shredded and the tomatoes sliced and gently slipped onto the dish. Mrs Higgs made the mayonnaise herself. She closeted herself in the pantry to do it, and we hardly dared breathe while that delicate operation was in progress.

SHAW THE VEGETARIAN

When Shaw was a young man of twenty-five, in 1881, scraping a living in London, he first became a vegetarian. In his words: 'I grew tired of beef and mutton, the steam and grease, the waiter looking as though he had been caught in a shower of gravy and not properly dried, the beer, the prevailing redness of nose, and the reek of the slaughterhouse that convicted us all of being beasts of prey. I fled to the purer air of the vegetarian restaurant.' And he discovered a number where it was possible to eat cheaply. He remained a vegetarian until his death seventy years later and believed that he was much healthier for it. He also believed that if everyone became vegetarian more people in the world could be properly fed. Violet says that Mr Shaw was perfectly satisfied to eat the vegetables Mrs Higgs provided and leave the meat or fish to Mrs Shaw and any visitors. He would add a note to invitation cards to dinner guests: 'My wife will provide a corpse.'

We used the best ingredients – brown sugar and plenty of cream, eggs and parsley to make our own sauces and soups. I usually made the tomato sauce, and in the days before blenders everything had to be put through a sieve, or several sieves. We had a wire sieve, a hair sieve and every other kind of sieve you can imagine. Mrs Higgs was never on my back, but even so I had to have my mind on the job and watch the clock, for example when the vegetables were cooking, because they had to be done just right. When it was spinach, I had to drain it off when it was cooked, then while it was still boiling hot I'd squeeze it from one hand to the other, to get rid of all the extra liquid, then put it in the vegetable dish.

TOMATO SAUCE

Violet's tomato sauce was often served with Mr Shaw's vegetables. First the butter was melted in a saucepan, then flour added and mixed thoroughly. A little of the tomato juice was used to thin the paste before mixing in the rest of the tomato pulp. The tomatoes had already been boiled, then put through a sieve – 'We did a lot of sieving,' Violet said, with feeling. Thyme, parsley and whole peppercorns were added at this stage of cooking and removed before serving.

We were supplied with our goods locally. First thing in the morning, when I came downstairs, there would be a little basket in the porch from the farm next door. They delivered milk, cream and eggs every day. The eggs we kept in a big stone crock in the larder. There was a shop in Welwyn that made sure that Mr Shaw had his lettuce and Mrs Shaw her grapes, whatever the time of year and come what may. Grapes cost a guinea a bunch at that time, I was told, and that was a lot of money then. On a Friday Mrs Higgs brought back fresh herrings from the village, and the way she cooked them they tasted out of this world!

Opposite the scullery door at Ayot there is a shed where the generator for the electricity was kept – and our bikes too. Built over that was a pigeon loft, and every now and then the pigeons were culled. A couple of dead birds would arrive in the scullery, and I would stand and look at them. Mrs Higgs would say, 'Now, you can never say you are trained if you don't know how to pluck a bird. So you will have to learn how to do it.' I used to poke at the thing first, to make sure it was really dead. I didn't really like the job at all, but I learned to pluck a bird – and to skin a rabbit – and it really did come in useful later on. If a brace of pheasants arrived, I knew what to do.

SHAW THE TEETOTALLER

Shaw's father was a heavy drinker, and as a boy Shaw had often seen the damaging results of alcohol. He himself was strictly teetotal. He believed that it was all right for most people to have a small amount of alcohol, but for those few who were 'leaders and geniuses' (which of course included himself) alcohol was out of the question because it would prevent them from reaching their highest possible achievement. There was never any alcohol in the house at Ayot, and Shaw himself drank water, barley-water, milk or a bland night-time milk drink – but hardly ever coffee and *never* tea.

The Temperance Societies of the time might have hoped to find a champion in Shaw. But to their disappointment he made fun of prohibition and mischievously pronounced that 'tea does more harm in the world than beer'. He even bought shares in a municipal public house because he said: 'Living is so painful for the poor, that it cannot be endured without an anaesthetic.'

I think it was recognised early on that waiting at table in the dining-room was what I was best suited for, and I had the opportunity to do that whenever Maggie was off duty. One thing I never did learn how to do at the Shaws' was to serve wine. Mr Shaw was strictly teetotal, and no wine was ever served in the house. But I owe everything else to Mrs Higgs who trained me so well. Her training was vital to me in days still to come, although what was going to happen to me later was beyond my wildest dreams.

4

SERVING THE GENTRY

Ayot is not a very big house. It had once been a rectory. But it was large enough for the staff to keep to their own separate quarters. Inside the front door is a large, square entrance hall and Mr Shaw's study; the drawing-room and the dining-room lead off the hall. At the back of the house a passageway led to the kitchen door and the backstairs. Upstairs was Mr Shaw's room, Mrs Shaw's room and the guest rooms. The other side of the landing was Mr and Mrs Higgs' bedroom and bathroom.

We used the back stairs, of course, and Maggie and I had to go up another flight of stairs to get to the attic, where our rooms were. Mine was a very sparse room with a single bed, wash-stand and dressing-table in white wood, and a cold linoleum floor. There was no heating. We used the lavatory on the next floor down, near the Higgs' bedroom, but we didn't have the use of a bathroom except on very rare occasions when there was no one else about. That meant we had to fetch jugs of hot water up all those stairs and wash in the basin on the washstand. We were provided with Lifebuoy soap – a large cake of red-coloured soap that smelt strongly of carbolic.

Washing my hair was the worst problem. There was so little water to spare that I could never rinse out the Amami shampoo properly, and that meant I suffered from dandruff. It was difficult to feel or look, or smell, nice. So one time on my half-day off I went to the little corner chemist's shop in the village and treated myself to some talcum powder – I think it was rose-scented. I hoped that a sprinkle of that on my skin after I'd washed might make me feel fresher and nicer. And would you believe it, Mrs Higgs stood at the bottom of the attic stairs and called up, 'What is that smell?'

As well as being exhausted with the heavy work I used to suffer dreadfully from indigestion. This went on for years and I had no idea what caused it. Then one day when Cook was dishing up the meal for the dining-room, I asked her if I could have a bit of potato to eat. And that solved my problem. You see we didn't have our meal until the dining-room had been served and cleared and I had been going too long without food.

We had one half-day off a week and one day a month and on Sundays we had either the morning or the evening off by turn. It always seemed to be raining on my day off. By the time lunch was over and we had finished eating our own meal and clearing everything up, it would be about three o'clock or even later, but it was no good hurrying to get ahead because half-day wasn't meant to begin until three. If I cycled home then it would be four o'clock before I arrived, but I had friends who lived just down the road. One had been my Sunday school teacher when I was younger, and the other, her friend, taught music. So most times I used to go to them for my half-day off, and they were very kind; I think they felt sorry for me. They encouraged me to play the piano and shared my enthusiasm that I should be a missionary. I still had that ambition. We used to be told at chapel that whatever our job, we could show our Christian faith by the way we did our work. But to me that wasn't the same as being a real missionary. When I had a Sunday morning off, I would go back to my old church and take a Sunday School class for anyone who was away or needed a Sunday off.

Ten o'clock at night was the deadline for getting back to Ayot. I'll never forget one particular evening after Clifford and I had been to the mid-week evening Prayer Meeting at

George Bernard Shaw in later years

the church. When we got home Dad insisted that Clifford should cycle back with me to Ayot, and one way and another it was two minutes past ten when we arrived. I burst into the kitchen, breathless, and Mrs Higgs was standing there waiting for me. She looked at me hard and said rather coldly, 'I hope this won't be a regular occurrence.' She did not need to say any more. I was never late again. I think that was the only occasion that Mrs Higgs had to tick me off.

The one time that I was off work for a while was when I had to go into hospital. Doing work 'the rough way' – on hands and knees – led to bursitis in one knee. It's not surprising that they used to call it 'housemaid's knee'. I was in hospital for several weeks, and in the end they had to operate.

On the Sunday after the operation the doctor came round the ward and asked how I was. I told him that my knee was still very painful, and he insisted on having a look at it himself. The ward sister did not look at all pleased at this, and she was very annoyed when Doctor told her that the knee should have

Mrs Shaw in later years

been put in a splint. But she had to follow his orders, and once the nurse put the splint on, the pain eased off and the knee began to heal.

That same afternoon Clifford came to visit me. He told me that the minister had prayed for me in church that morning, so I asked him what time that had been. And it turned out that the very time the minister prayed for me was just when the doctor looked at my knee and found the cause of the trouble.

When I got back to Ayot St Lawrence I had another surprise. Mrs Shaw came into the kitchen, carrying a cushion with a long handle attached. 'Perhaps you would like this,' she said and handed it to me to use when I did the rough work on my hands and knees.

I was completely taken aback. It wasn't like Mrs Shaw to think of something like that, and I could see that Mrs Higgs was really moved by Mrs Shaw's kindness. But I was not expected to show my feelings or say anything except, 'Thank you very much, Madam.'

Plenty is known and said about Mr Shaw, but Mrs Shaw was a private and retiring lady; she did not like the spotlight in any way. I learned to respect that and to be discreet. She had been a lady in her own right and had a wonderfully full life before her marriage. She was intellectual too. She always dressed beautifully and walked slowly. She was very ladylike and dignified in her manner. There was never any confrontation of any kind between her and Mr Shaw. He treated her with respect and courtesy, and she did the same to him. It was a peaceful house and Mrs Shaw did not like any kind of contention. In fact it was an orderly, well-regulated house. Whatever might have gone on, there was no hint of anything improper in the house.

I always got on all right with Mrs Shaw and tried to follow Mrs Higgs' instructions: 'Just do everything properly and don't give her any cause to complain because if you do I shall hear about it for weeks.'

Mrs Shaw did reprimand me once – about a mustard pot that was not quite clean. (When the table was cleared, the mustard had to be emptied out and the pot washed; then the mustard was put back in a clean pot.) After that I made quite sure that the cruets were spotless – and have done so to this day.

But I think she must have approved of me in general because when Mrs Higgs told her that I wanted to be a missionary, she said, 'Not yet, I hope.' That was her way of saying that she did not want to lose me – I suited her – and that was a real compliment.

Mrs Higgs was very close to Mrs Shaw, and Mr Shaw thought a lot of Mr Higgs. But the rest of us absorbed impressions rather than hearing much inside information about the Shaws and their visitors. I got on well with the rest of the staff, but it wasn't the custom to chat or gossip among ourselves. We would never discuss our employers or say things like, 'I wonder what mood she'll be in today' or even talk about what we'd done on our day off. I had a friend who had a job in a work-room, where they sewed clothes, and she said the same thing. They were expected to get on quietly and not chatter.

Then again, I met Arthur Inch when we were both advising on the *Gosford Park* film and he had been a butler at big houses, including Blenheim Palace. He has quite another story to tell. He said the servants gossiped about everything, and that included the gentry upstairs as well as what they'd all got up to on their days off. So perhaps it was because we were a small staff and Mrs Higgs had such consideration for Mrs Shaw that it wasn't like that at Ayot.

It was strange really what a real mix we were in that household – and we all got on well. Mrs Higgs was Church of England, Maggie was Roman Catholic, Miss Patch was the daughter of a vicar and I was Baptist. Mrs Higgs passed on very little, but she did say that Mrs Shaw had told her that she used to sing hymns at her mother's knee.

As staff we were trusted completely. You hear stories about employers who put a shilling under the rug to test their servants' honesty, but there was never anything of the kind with us. It was usually accepted that it was only 'cheap' employers who behaved like that – not the real gentry. As my grandmother used to say, 'We kept our feet under *gentlemen's* tables.' She meant that we worked for the nobility who knew how to behave, not jumped-up newcomers to money and position.

Not long before I left, I did stick up for myself on one occasion, and it led to a bit of a set-to with Maggie. As I have explained, Maggie cleared the dining-room fire, and I did the one in the drawing-room. One day I happened to go into the dining-room while Maggie was clearing the fire and couldn't believe my eyes. She was poking the fire with *my* poker, for my use in the drawing room. No wonder it got so black and needed cleaning so often! You see, the ornamental poker in each room was not for us to use – just the lady of the house if she wanted to poke the fire. But Maggie and I each had an old poker of our own to take round with us. All the pokers had to be properly cleaned with emery paper and I had noticed how quickly mine seemed to need cleaning – not surprising! I didn't make a scene when I caught Maggie using it, but I did let it be known that I was not pleased.

When people ask about my hobbies and interests at that time, I don't think they realise how little energy or scope there was for anything outside work. I was exhausted when I did come off duty, and beyond joining in church activities when I could, I didn't embark on much else except that I got started on a Home Preparation Course for missionary work. I still cherished my ambition.

Looking back now, I realise that I was always having to fight exhaustion and lack of energy. In those days you had to struggle on; no one really wanted to know or look into such things. On one occasion I was cleaning in T. E. Lawrence's room, and I literally did not know how I was going to get another ounce of energy to go on to the next patch of floor. I just begged God to help me.

LAWRENCE OF ARABIA (1888–1935)

As a student at Oxford, Thomas Edward Lawrence completed a solitary walk of 1,100 miles in the Middle East and later learned the language and culture of the Arabs. When war broke out in 1914, he became a British agent in the Middle East, reporting on Germany's allies, the Turks. But he longed passionately to free his Arab friends from centuries of Turkish domination and began to lead guerrilla warfare on their behalf.

His reputation for bravery and panache earned him international fame as 'Lawrence of Arabia'. Dressed in flowing Arab robes, at the head of a galloping horse-back army, he finally seized the vital port of Aqaba from the Turks, without firing a shot.

Shaw was one of Lawrence's heroes. When they met in 1922 he gave Shaw a copy of his memoirs, *The Seven Pillars of Wisdom*. Shaw pronounced it one of the great books of the world. Charlotte proof-read it and was awe-struck.

A strong friendship grew up between Charlotte and Lawrence. She loaded him with exotic gifts, and the Shaws gave Lawrence his first motorbike – a powerful machine that he called Boanerges. He would roar up to Ayot, unannounced, in his goggles and gauntlets and peaked cap, sometimes staying in the 'Lawrence room' that Violet remembers so well.

In 1935, the Shaws were abroad when news reached them of Lawrence's death. He was riding his motorbike back from the airfield when he skidded to avoid two boys on bikes, shot over the handle bars and was instantly killed. Charlotte never forgot him, for he was, as she put it, 'the strangest contact in my life'.

T. E. Lawrence was one visitor I never met, although his presence still seemed to linger in the house. I first heard about this gentleman at school, during my last term. One morning we were summoned to the school hall for a solemn announcement to be made. We were told that if we lived in the Ayot area we had probably noticed a young man who rode around on a motorbike. His name was T. E. Lawrence and he had just been killed in a motor-cycle crash. When I went to the Shaws'

I found that he had been a close friend of theirs and had visited them often.

Mrs Shaw never referred to him; I think it upset her to talk about him. Certainly the room where he used to stay was always kept as it had been and cleaned regularly; it was referred to as his room and never used for any other guests. There was a shelf of his books in the drawing-room, and I used to say I'd read T. E. Lawrence, because I'd dusted them so often.

BEATRICE WEBB

Born in 1858, Beatrice was the eighth daughter of Richard Potter, a wealthy businessman. Unusually for the period, Mr Potter treated his daughters as friends and equals. He tutored Beatrice, who was an avid reader and grew up to be a handsome and formidable woman with a large annuity. Herbert Spencer was one of her many suitors.

Although Beatrice was raised with great privilege, what she learned about working-class life from one of her favourite nannies revolutionised her thinking. Although she rather despised the Fabians at first for their fads and foibles, she later joined them and married their founder, Sidney Webb. They were devoted to each other during fifty years of happy, though childless, marriage.

The Webbs founded the London School of Economics, which was intended to spread the Fabian gospel, and in 1912 they published the *New Statesman* journal, which has stayed true to Fabian ideals ever since.

FABIAN SOCIETY

In 1886 Sidney Webb founded the Fabian Society, which aimed to bring about 'democratic socialism'. Some members were Christians, like Charles Kingsley, the reforming clergyman who wrote *The Water Babies*. Others, like philosopher Bertrand Russell, were self-confessed atheists. But all aimed to bring about better conditions for the poor and under-privileged.

In spite of being good socialists, most members of the Society were middle-class intellectuals. Socialism, they realised, must come to Britain gradually, and it was sixty years before the Labour Government, voted in at the 1945 election, put the Fabian ideals and plans into action.

SHAW AND THE FABIANS

Bernard Shaw was attracted to the Society's aims. He became – and remained – a leading light in the Society. He added a pencilled note to the minutes of the first Fabian meeting that he attended, which read: 'This meeting was made memorable by the first appearance of Bernard Shaw.'

Shaw's plays and articles expressed his socialist ideals. He was tireless in speaking on behalf of his beliefs. Shaw never took any money for these speeches even though he was very poor at the time. He could hold audiences spellbound and even captured the interest of the stony-faced policeman sent to watch him when he was speaking in Hyde Park. Many of the early Fabians, such as Sidney and Beatrice Webb, became close friends of the Shaws and were among the visitors that Violet remembers.

Due to Mrs Shaw's poor health, not many visitors came to stay at Ayot. Lord Sidney and Lady Beatrice Webb would come to stay – there was a guest room with two beds next to Mrs Shaw's room where they slept, but like other visitors, they didn't really cross our paths. They drifted around, but our job was to get the work done quickly and thoroughly and vacate the rooms before they appeared. In that way guests and staff would not cross paths, and we would not be seen or heard.

WEEKENDS AT CLIVEDEN

Cliveden overlooks a lovely stretch of the River Thames and is conveniently near to Windsor and London. It was built in 1660 and restored in the nineteenth century by Sir Charles Barry, the famous architect who designed the Houses of Parliament. In 1893 the Duke of Westminster sold the whole property to William Waldorf Astor the American multimillionaire who gave it as a wedding present to his son Waldorf and wife, Nancy.

Nancy filled the house with flowers and replaced stuffy house parties with action-packed weekends, attended by royalty, politicians and literary figures too. The Shaws were frequent guests. Winston Churchill, Nancy complained, sulked if he was not seated next to someone he liked at dinner. The two feuded constantly.

> Nancy once told Winston, 'If you were my husband I'd put poison in your coffee,' to which he replied, 'If you were my wife I'd drink it.'

Mrs Shaw did not go out much socially. But Cliveden, the big country house owned by Lady Nancy Astor, was nearby and Mr and Mrs Shaw visited there, and Lady Astor used to come to see Mrs Shaw at Ayot. She was a breath of fresh air, sweeping in the door and whirling up the stairs to see Mrs Shaw, if she was not up yet. But it seems she still had time to notice the stairs because Mrs Shaw said to me once, 'Lady Astor remarked on how nice the stairs looked.' This was praise indeed and it made up for all my hard work.

NANCY ASTOR

She was born Nancy Langhorne in Danville, Virginia, in the United States and remained a true Virginian all her days. Though only five foot two, she made up in energy and high spirits what she lacked in size. Bernard Shaw commented that she could never think consecutively for sixty seconds, but as the first woman Member of Parliament to take her seat in the House of Commons, she could plead her causes persuasively and enter into the cut and thrust of debate with gusto. She championed women and children and the poor – nursery schools, cheap milk, slum clearance and equal pay for men and women were some of her causes.

After the death of Charlotte, Nancy tried to take Bernard Shaw under her wing, but Shaw would have none of it. 'Keep off! Keep off! Keep off! Keep off!' he told her, 'upset your own household, not mine. In this house what I say goes.'

When Nancy died in 1964 a Confederate flag from the American Civil War covered the casket containing her ashes. They were interred, with Waldorf's ashes, in the chapel at Cliveden.

My favourite visitor was Mrs Angela Cherry-Garrard. She and her husband lived nearby and would often walk across for Sunday lunch. She was a lovely person and so kind to Mrs Shaw, who loved her. She always brought Mrs Shaw a bunch of sweet-smelling Parma violets, which would be arranged in a little vase and put on a wooden fretwork stand on the same little table in the drawing-room. I don't think dear Mrs Cherry-Garrard realised what it meant to us that they always arrived late. If lunch was not punctual it meant that we were late clearing up and if it was your turn to have Sunday afternoon off, you didn't get off duty until even later than usual.

AYOT ST LAWRENCE, WELWYN, HERTS.
STATION: WHEATHAMPSTEAD, L&N.E.R, 2¼ MILES.
TELEGRAMS: BERNARD SHAW, CODICOTE.
TELEPHONE: CODICOTE 218.

From Bernard Shaw.

4, WHITEHALL COURT (130) LONDON, S.W.1.
PHONE: WHITEHALL 3160.
TELEGRAMS: SOCIALIST, PARL-LONDON.

21st June 1944

Miss Violet Pond was in my domestic service and that of my late wife as housemaid and assistant parlormaid for six years until she was called up for war work in 1943. She was efficient in her duties, irreproachable in her conduct, and gave no trouble of any kind.

G. Bernard Shaw

Reference for Violet from Bernard Shaw

APSLEY AND ANGELA CHERRY-GARRARD

Apsley Cherry-Garrard – known to friends as 'Cherry' – inherited the family estate at Lamer, not far from Shaw's Corner. Although in awe of his famous neighbour, Bernard Shaw, Cherry and his wife, Angela, became close friends of the Shaws. Soon Shaw was advising him on the manuscript of his book, *The Worst Journey in the World*, an account of Scott's last Antarctic expedition.

As a young admirer of Captain Scott, Cherry had volunteered for the expedition, which had left him scarred for life, both emotionally and physically. It was Cherry's small party, in fact, that had discovered Scott and his companions frozen to death in their tents. Soon after, Cherry was drafted to serve at the front lines of World War I, where he was wounded.

At fifty-three, Cherry married Angela, thirty years his junior, at a time when World War II was looming. Although Cherry suffered terrible, undeserved remorse, believing that he might have prevented Scott's tragic ending, he and Angela were wonderfully happy together, and she nurtured and nursed him for the rest of his troubled life. Everyone loved Angela, and she entered into the life of the village and church. On Sundays, as Violet recalled, Cherry and Angela would stroll over for Sunday lunch, and on Wednesdays the Shaws went across to Lamer to lunch with the Cherry-Garrards.

I can remember waiting for them to arrive but not daring to look at the clock, because if Mrs Higgs caught you doing that she immediately found an extra job for you to do. They'd saunter in eventually, and we were ready to serve lunch as soon as possible after that.

Dame Wendy Hiller, the actress, used to come to see Mr Shaw, and she'd be ushered into his study. I believe it was to talk about a film she was in, which was based on one of his plays, either *Pygmalion* or *Major Barbara*, I'm not sure which. I think he asked for her to be in it because she was one of his favourite actresses. I do remember that some time after that Mrs Higgs said, 'We are going to Harpenden today to see the film,' and off we went to see *Major Barbara*. She didn't say why we were going or who had paid for the tickets for us to go, and I can't say I enjoyed it or understood much.

After writing all morning Mr Shaw would come to sit with Mrs Shaw for a while before they went in to lunch together. After lunch he'd have his rest. Visitors to Shaw's Corner now are told that he rested on the couch in his study, where the papers were, but he certainly never did this while I was there. He used a more comfortable couch in the dining-room.

Sometimes in the afternoon Mr and Mrs Shaw would walk round the garden together, marking each lap, as they completed it, with a pebble that they would place on the little wall by the house. Later on Mrs Shaw was not able to walk far, and Mr Shaw would go on his own around the drive, swinging his stick, while Reggie, their little dog, stood at the front door where he could watch both gates at opposite ends of the drive and keep guard. Although Reggie was their dog, Mrs Shaw would often get tired of having him around. When that happened the kitchen door would open and Mrs Shaw would call out, 'Mrs Higgs! Mrs Higgs!' That was all that was said, but we knew what it meant. The next moment Reggie would come running in through the door and go straight to Mrs Higgs. I think he preferred being her dog to being Mrs Shaw's.

Mrs Shaw was already unwell when I first started at Ayot. It must have been after she had had scarlet fever because I'm told that was when she began to decline. She suffered from arthritis and her bones deteriorated, and I could tell that she was failing. Of course, these days the doctors might have been able to do more. Later on a special chair was ordered, recommended by the doctor. It's still there in the drawing-room at Shaw's Corner, but what I called the 'rollie' cushion is missing. I know very well that there were three cushions for me to plump up and that the little sausage-shaped one for her neck and head has disappeared now. Mrs Shaw grew weaker, but she was in London when she finally died.

MRS SHAW'S ILLNESS AND DEATH

Mrs Shaw's health began to fail, and as her condition grew worse, she longed to escape from Ayot, which she described as her 'little prison'. So, in the summer of 1943, on his eighty-seventh birthday, Shaw drove her back to London, to Whitehall Court, where she grew gradually weaker. Then, one day in September, Shaw noticed a change. She seemed to look young again, as he first remembered her. She remained this way, he told friends, until her death a few days later.

Mrs Shaw had requested: 'no flowers, no black clothes, no service', so a brief cremation took place at Golders Green crematorium attended only by Bernard Shaw himself, Lady Astor and Miss Patch. Charlotte had originally requested that her ashes should be 'scattered on Irish soil', but when the war started Shaw suggested that their ashes should be mixed together and scattered around the garden at Ayot. 'It pleased her,' he said, 'and she agreed.' So Charlotte's ashes were left in a bronze casket at Golders Green, to await her husband's death.

Mr Shaw had a great deal of charm but it never seemed artificial or came over as if he didn't mean it. He certainly never exerted his authority or complained about anything, even after Mrs Shaw died. He had a beautiful way of saying my name, and I used to linger at the bottom of the stairs in the morning, dusting the telephone far longer than need be, so that I could hear him say my name when he came downstairs. He'd say, 'Good morning, Vi-o-let' with such a lovely Irish lilt to his voice.

MAISKY'S FAREWELL

Ivan Maisky had been a frequent visitor to the Shaws' house during his eleven-year stay in Britain as Ambassador from the USSR. In his *Memoirs of a Soviet Ambassador*, he wrote of Mrs Shaw's illness: 'In her early youth she had been thrown by a horse, and had injured her spine.... At the age of ninety, Charlotte Shaw was a complete invalid: her frame was bent, she could not raise her head and spent the whole day in bed. But on our farewell visit she rose, dressed, and came down into the drawing-room. She wished us the best in life and recalled with deep satisfaction our eleven years' friendship....

'The end came earlier than we could have expected. On the very day of our departure, an hour before the train left, we learned that Charlotte was dead. The first impulse was to go to Bernard Shaw and personally express our deep sympathy, but this was impossible: in wartime conditions one could not even think of postponing departure even for a few hours. Then I took a sheet of paper, and in a few heartfelt lines expressed all our grief and shock at the loss he had suffered. . . .'

Sometimes Miss Patch, his secretary who moved down from London, would be following behind him. She would bark out 'Good morning!' in such a gruff tone, it was a complete contrast. But she had a responsible job and did it well and she lived in her own different world. We never crossed swords, but I can't say that she exactly endeared herself to us. Poor Miss Patch!

MISS PATCH

'Would you care to be my secretary?' Shaw asked forty-year-old Blanche Patch, a clergyman's daughter who had been a nurse and was at that time a typist. Charlotte was pleasantly impressed with her, but Blanche took some persuading. At first she was nervous and asked one of the servants: 'Does he throw things at you?' But she stayed with Bernard Shaw from 1920 until his death thirty years later.

She had little sense of humour and was unimpressed by Shaw as a writer. Still, she efficiently transcribed the

fifteen hundred words he had written in his own pho-
netic shorthand every day from the green-tinted paper
he wrote on – to rest his eyes. She was firm to those who
tried to intrude on Shaw's time and was often addressed
as 'Miss Cross Patch', but, in fact, it was Shaw himself
who irritated her most. 'Go away and write another
play!' she would exclaim, when his pacing brought him
near her desk.

In his will he left her an annuity of £500, a handsome
sum at that time. She always treasured the fact that he
once referred to her as 'The faithful Patch'.

Mr Shaw was very musical, in fact he had been a music critic
at one time, Mrs Higgs told us. There was no wireless in the
kitchen, but if I was clearing the dining-room I would see him
listening intently to the music. Mrs Higgs said, 'You know he's
a critic, and if he hears a wrong note he'll ring up the BBC and
tell them,' and I thought how clever it was to be able to pick
out one wrong note in all that marvellous musical harmony.

He would sometimes play the piano in the evenings, he
was a very good pianist. Mrs Shaw would be lying in bed and
could listen to him. And sometimes Mrs Higgs would sum-
mon us to the top landing – it wasn't very big – but we could
stand there, quiet as mice, and hear him play in the hall below.
(We mustn't be seen or heard, of course.) He never thumped
or played loudly – Mrs Shaw could not have stood that – but
his playing was somehow feathery, that's the only way I can
describe it.

It was my job to dust and clean Mr Shaw's study and there
were always four piles of papers on the couch there. They

Photo of Violet taken by Bernard Shaw

never seemed to change, as I know because I dusted them each day. But as for reading them or looking closely at them – I knew I must not start doing that. So although I'm so fond of books and always have been, I had to curb my curiosity. If I'd started reading I'd have found it hard to stop so I knew I must not begin because if I was caught I would lose my job.

One day Mrs Shaw came along when I was answering the phone, which was outside the study. Some reporters were on the line, and I gave the usual kind of answer to put them off. Mrs Shaw thought that I had spoken to them unwisely and told me so. To my surprise, Mr Shaw opened his study door and said quietly and firmly, 'Violet did not.' No more was said, and Mrs Shaw just walked away. I was told that he had stood up for a member of staff in the same way once before.

Mr Shaw was very keen on photography, and one evening, out of the blue, he called me into the dining-room. He told me to take my cap off and said that he wanted to take my photograph. You can imagine how pleased I was, but I knew I must compose myself and not show my feelings when I went back to the kitchen. He had never taken Maggie's photo, and I guessed what the atmosphere would be like if I looked like the cat that got the cream. But I still treasure that photo.

I know people have the ready-made idea that Mr Shaw was an atheist, and they frown at me when I try to say otherwise. I can only say that from what I saw and knew of him I feel sure that although he may not have believed in the way that I do, he still had a faith of his own. I believe that there were only four people at Mrs Shaw's funeral at the crematorium, and they included Miss Patch and Lady Astor. I'm told that when they played 'I Know That My Redeemer Liveth', Mr Shaw sang the words. I am sure that he would never have done that if he hadn't believed in the truth of it. He just wasn't that kind of man.

Soon after Mrs Shaw's death, Mr Shaw saw me in the hall and called me across. He took a five pound note out of his pocket and said that he wanted to give it to me as from Mrs Shaw.

I was so taken aback that I just managed to blurt out, 'I only did my duty, sir.'

He replied, 'Duty as you have done it, Violet, ceases to be duty.'

I was so overcome that I just fled to the kitchen.

But I was finding the work increasingly exhausting and didn't know how long I could go on. One day – I was twenty-one by then – when no one else was about, I literally knelt on the kitchen floor – I can remember the exact spot – and cried out to God, 'Lord, how long?' You see I felt that life was passing me by. Would there be nothing for me beyond Ayot?

Not long after that, however, a new chapter in my life did begin. I had not realised at the time that Mrs Shaw's death was going to lead to a startling and unexpected change in my whole life.

JOINING THE ARMY

*W*e were all very sad when Mrs Shaw died, and I certainly had no idea at that time that it would turn my life upside down. I was to be uprooted from the gentle calm of Ayot to take my place in the big wide world.

Up to now my call-up had been deferred because I was helping to look after two elderly people. But it soon became clear that now that Mrs Shaw had died and Mr Shaw was on his own, the authorities considered that Mrs Higgs and Maggie were quite able to manage without my help. So I had to leave not only Ayot, but also, for the first time, that part of the world where my family lived and which I knew and loved so well. I was to be called up into the Army.

I joined the ATS, as the women's branch of the Army was known then, at the end of 1943, and was ordered to Pontefract in Yorkshire to do my basic training. It was January and we were in the depths of winter cold. However *did* I survive? As a soft southerner used to the gentler climate of Buckinghamshire, Pontefract struck bitterly cold and exposed. It is in the northern county of Yorkshire, and that winter was a raw, bleak one. Much of the time we were confined to barracks, and life was a round of drill, exercises and a succession of jabs to inoculate us against various diseases we might come in contact with during army life.

ARMY UNIFORM

In 1941 clothes were rationed. Coupons were issued and somehow had to be stretched to buy necessary items. Some civilians complained: 'At least the service women get something decent to wear.' The kit Violet would have been issued with on joining up included: One cape/groundsheet, greatcoat, respirator, steel helmet, cap with badge, two jackets, two skirts, two brassieres, two suspender belts (or two corselettes to women of bust size 40–44), two blue overalls and buttons, button-stick, two tins anti-gas ointment and about another thirty items.

We had to line up out of doors in the freezing cold for our meals. Queuing for breakfast early in the morning was the worst. I did what I used to do at school, which was to get to the very back of the queue where I hoped I wouldn't be noticed. That's how I met Dorothy, who used to do the same. She became a real friend, and as she knew her way around better than I did, I'm sure she was more help to me than I was to her. I think she saw me as an innocent abroad and felt I needed to be looked after. Even after we were posted she sent a card to my mother to check that I was all right.

During the day we had to take part in army exercises. I remember one where we had to practise being under a gas attack. They pronounced me dead because I didn't react quickly enough. We marched a lot, of course, but I didn't mind that, even though the sergeant used to bellow at us to go on marching even when there was a brick wall straight ahead of us.

An old cutting of Violet and her brother, Clifford, in military uniform

After one of our sessions of training we were all huddled in the barrack room, wet through and shivering with cold. On top of that, we were still feeling ill from the different inoculations we'd been given. Just then the commanding officer came in, took one look at us and realised what a bad way we were in. She immediately gave the order, 'Put the heating on at once or I will not be responsible for these girls.'

One Sunday when we were allowed out, a few of us went to see Pontefract Castle. It looked bleak and grim in the cold winter light, a really depressing sight, but suddenly, I looked down and saw a crocus in bloom. My heart just leaped with joy – it seemed like a sign of hope and of God's goodness and care.

PONTEFRACT CASTLE

It's not surprising that Violet viewed the ruins of Ponte-fract Castle in gloomy mood. The castle has a sad and bloody history. It was built in the eleventh century by

Ilbert de Lacy, a loyal follower of William the Conqueror, but over the centuries the castle witnessed scenes of great cruelty. King Richard II was imprisoned and died there – or, as some have it, was murdered.

In the seventeenth century, during the Civil War, Pontefract Castle was the last remaining Royalist stronghold to be taken, and, as a result, the people of Pontefract suffered terribly. So when the war was over, the citizens of Pontefract asked for the Castle to be demolished, and it was reduced to the ruins to be seen today, where it has become a lively and attractive tourist centre.

Before I left home to join up, my father had said, 'Do as your brother has done and get in touch with the nearest church' (Clifford had already joined up in the RAF). One day I was scanning the notice board and saw that there was a service to be held that evening by SASRA (Soldiers' and Airmen's Scripture Readers' Association). I was off duty, so I decided to try to find out where it was going to be held and go along to it.

SASRA

Living where Servicemen and women are stationed, the members of the Soldiers' and Airmen's Scripture Readers' Association – known as missionaries in khaki and blue – aim to help people in the Forces to form a relationship with God. They also support those who are already Christians by putting them in touch with churches, as Violet discovered. Readers are free to go in and meet the men and women informally in their barracks and supplement the work of official Church of England and Roman Catholic chaplains, with whom they have a good working relationship.

I wandered around the whole barracks complex, trying to find the place, then, very faintly, I heard the sound of a harmonium, and it was playing hymn tunes that I recognised. That seemed hopeful, so I set off to follow the sound, knowing I was getting warmer as the sound got louder. I tracked down the room at last and went in. A Scripture Reader was sitting there, all on his own, playing the harmonium. He must have been pleased to have a congregation, even if it *was* only of one, and once we had introduced ourselves to each other, he took the service.

Afterwards he suggested that if I was not on PAD (Passive Air Defence) duty the next Sunday, he would take me to a Baptist Church. Sure enough I was free and set off, much to the surprise and consternation of the other girls in the Barrack Room. 'Going to church?' they asked incredulously. As I left I was accompanied by wolf whistles from the guards at the gates.

The Scripture Reader told me that he was taking services at the Methodist Church that day so he would leave me in the care of some friends of his who were Baptists and who would take me to their church. He'd fetch me again at the end of the day. When we arrived at the cottage where they lived, he knocked on the door. Then he turned to me and said, 'Follow me, I know these people.' He gently lifted the latch and, rather hesitantly, I followed him, straight into a little living-room where a couple were on their knees, praying. We knelt too and joined them. I shall always cherish the quietness and peace and holiness of that time.

When I arrived back that evening and went into the barrack room the other girls were amazed to see me smiling and radiant. The corporal said, 'Do you mean to tell us that you've been to church all day and you've got a face like that?' She seemed to think I ought to be glum and miserable-looking instead of feeling full of new strength and happiness. They were envious that I'd been invited into people's homes, but when I told them that if they went to church they'd get invited out too, there were no takers.

I later learned that the Army Scripture Reader and his wife had recently lost a son. They were very kind and gentle with me and so was the Church of England chaplain. He and his wife would put on a favourite chorus of mine whenever I went to their home. These Christian friends lighted up the bleakness of those first weeks of army life and helped me to get over the shock of such a change.

The time came for postings to be decided and we were able to choose whether to stay in this country or be posted abroad. Here was my chance. I opted for overseas, so – guess what? – I got a home posting, to Knightsbridge Barracks in London. So along with a bunch of other girls who joined up when I did, I travelled by train to London. But when the others went off to their own separate postings I was left alone on the station in the midst of a swirling crowd of people, feeling very much the raw recruit. So what to do next?

I remembered the well-known advice, 'If you want to know the way, ask a policeman.' And there, right on cue, I saw one, standing nearby, so that's just what I did. 'I've been posted to Knightsbridge Barracks,' I told him, 'and I don't know how to get there. Can you tell me?' Of course he could and kindly did, and so I picked up my kit bag and began the next stage of my journey.

I think I must have looked a bit of a poor fish when at last I arrived and walked in, because the girls were all very kind to me. Then it turned out that I was not to be stationed at the Barracks after all but at an army sick-bay at Moray Lodge, which was opposite Camden Hill and next to Barker's, the department store. They offered to take me there, and when I realised I'd left my kit bag behind in my nervousness and confusion, they even went back and fetched it for me.

I discovered that Moray Lodge had been a private house before being taken over for the war. I think that Ellen Terry, the famous actress, had once lived there. It was a beautiful house and unexpectedly there was a garden at the back so green and peaceful that it was like being in the heart of the country. Now, I'm afraid, it has been replaced by blocks of flats. But during the war the house was a sick bay in the care of Red Cross nurses and run by a Sister, who belonged to the Queen Alexandra Imperial Nursing Service. She was the only Captain there, and I was to be her bat-woman, but since I should have had several officers to look after instead of one, I had to combine my duties for her with helping as a sick bay orderly.

MORAY LODGE

When Violet was posted to Moray Lodge she heard that it had once been the home of Ellen Terry. But although Ellen Terry, the famous actress and close friend of Bernard Shaw, visited the house, it had belonged to her older sister Kate. Both sisters made their stage debut at a tender age, as three- and four-year- olds, and when they grew older Kate looked set to eclipse Ellen on the stage.

Arthur Lewis, the son of a wealthy merchant, had moved to Moray Lodge from his bachelor apartments in London's Jermyn Street. He entertained widely and formed his own band known as the Moray Minstrels. Lewis planned to put on a performance of Sullivan's operetta *Cox and Box*, staged first at Moray Lodge. He invited both Ellen and Kate to take part in it, but it was Kate, not Ellen, who married Lewis and became mistress of Moray Lodge. She retired from the stage, leaving Ellen as undisputed queen.

QUEEN ALEXANDRA IMPERIAL NURSING SERVICE

In 1902 Queen Alexandra, wife of Edward VII, became patron of the reorganised army nursing services and gave her name to the band of trained nurses who served as officers in the British Army. Henceforward they would be known as Queen Alexandra's Imperial Military Nursing Service – QAs for short.

When I was free in the evenings I would go along to a Christian club run by two ladies who had been missionaries. Once again my piano-playing came in useful, and I would often play for the services they held and for the community hymn-singing that followed. The ladies said they liked it when it was my turn to play because I knew when to call a halt to the proceedings after the service. Poor things! They still had to clear up before they could go home themselves, and you can guess why they didn't want to finish too late. They weren't as young as we all were, and they were tired out.

My favourite visitors to the club were the American soldiers. You could hear them coming a mile off. They'd be singing hymns as they came along the street, and they were so polite and friendly as well as being warm and cheerful. It didn't matter if they were officers and we were just privates or corporals. They'd take our coats for us and offer us a seat and be so charming and full of fun. There was never any side with them.

I had two different boyfriends during this time. One was Dutch, and he was billeted at the back of the Albert Hall. He had lost all his family in the war, and he was a quiet chap but very clever especially with languages.

But my first boyfriend was Fred. He was a Methodist. Sadly he got posted away, I think with the Eighth Army, while I was in St George's hospital for a while. (The constant bombing had affected my health.) Anyway, he didn't know where I was or what had become of me, and although he left a message, we lost touch. That was the end of that. It was because everything about postings and the whereabouts of service personnel was so hush-hush that no one was supposed to know exactly where anyone was sent. For quite a while I used to think that perhaps he would turn up again, but he never did.

One day, when the London bombing began again, a bomb fell on the London School of Economics, and Moray Lodge caught the blast. Captain shouted, 'Come away from the window, Pond!' There was a sound of shattering glass, and she and I clung to one another as falling plaster and rubble threw up clouds of smothering dust all around us. At that moment a verse from the Bible flashed into my mind: 'Wherever you are, the Lord your God is with you.'

THE HIGGSES LEAVE AYOT

In 1944, after Mrs Shaw's death and when the doodle-bugs were causing havoc in London, the Higgses felt that they must give in their notice and retire. Shaw described his emotions when they finally left Ayot, in a letter to Lady Astor: 'They went away in a handsome cab, beautifully dressed, with the dog on its lead, greatly excited. I kissed her goodbye, and waved after them until the car disappeared round the corner. . . . When I went to the shelter to write, I found that my pen wobbled a little in my hand.'

We both survived that incident, but there was a sad sequel for Sister. A bomb fell when she was waiting at traffic lights in Earls Court, and she and everyone there was killed outright. It was a tense time, and when our officer showed us a map of London and explained that Hitler intended to wipe out the whole of Kensington, I thought, 'There's not much hope for us is there?' My spirits were low.

I think we were all pretty stressed at this time, with the incessant bombing, the constant danger and the tragic losses. I can remember taking tea and coffee to the medical staff one day and a really nice doctor, who had always been so pleasant and friendly, suddenly screamed at me and shouted a stream of abuse. I fled from the room, but one of the staff followed me out and told me not to take any notice of the outburst. It was a result of the stress. That particular doctor was not the only one who had to be given sick leave on the grounds of nervous exhaustion and breakdown.

One day when Moray Lodge caught the worst of the bomb damage, we were told that we would have to spend the night in some kind of shelter while temporary repairs were done to the building. We lined up at a depot where the staff, rather looking down their noses at us, handed us our blankets, one apiece, and told us to march to the emergency shelter. This turned out to be the basement of an old Victorian house. It was completely bare except for two bunks, and there were five or six of us from Moray Lodge who had to bed down there for the night. I remember feeling really sorry for myself. I wondered if there was anyone who knew where we were, to come and rescue us if a bomb should fall.

It was a long, restless night in that shelter as we heard the bombs falling all around. As soon as I could, while it was still early, I made my escape as quietly as possible and set off to walk back to Moray Lodge. When I got as far as Kensington Barracks one of the guards barred my way.

'Where do you think you are going?' he asked. When I told him that I was going to Moray Lodge he went off and made a phone call and came back looking grim. 'I don't think you'd better go,' he said, but I refused to be put off and insisted on finishing my journey. 'Well, watch how you go then,' he said and reluctantly let me pass.

As I came nearer Moray Lodge I could see that another bomb had destroyed all the temporary repairs to the house. The emergency fabric that had been covering the windows was shredded and flapping in the breeze. It was a sorry sight.

Eventually, when everyone else had turned up, we were told to meet in the main downstairs room. It had once been such a beautiful room, the best in this once-lovely house. Now it was laid waste, everything covered in dust and rubble We were told that we were to have a few days' compassionate sick leave. Still dazed and in a bit of a dream, I made my way home to Mum and Dad. I felt a bit like a drowned rat, and I think I must have looked like one because that was the first time that I can remember my parents showing real concern for me. It was the first time too that I had seen fear in my father's eyes. He realised how much danger I was in. I suppose I must have known deep down that they loved me, but I could only guess at it from hints and signs like that.

It was during this leave that I got on my bike and cycled back to Ayot. I don't know now what got into me. I suppose I wanted to forget the nightmare of the present and remember the past. Mrs Higgs had left by this time, and someone called Mrs Laden was looking after Mr Shaw. When she found out who I was she said, 'Go down and see him – go on!'

Mr Shaw was in his garden house writing at the time, and I went in fear and trepidation because it was unheard of to disturb him. But he received me so courteously and said in his soft Irish voice, 'May I ask where you are posted?'

So I said, 'Oh, yes, sir,' and then I told him about the London School of Economics being bombed and how we caught the blast. He was interested to hear that, of course, because Mrs Shaw's flat had once been there. That was the last time I saw him.

ALICE LADEN

Mrs Alice Laden was a grey-haired, pink-cheeked widow with a strong Aberdonian accent. She arrived with her marmalade cat in a basket, and took over. 'I want you to look after me till I die,' Shaw had told her. She was an out-and-out Tory and told Mr Shaw that she thoroughly disapproved of his Socialist views. He seemed to enjoy her outspokenness. But she stood no nonsense from him, and he was not allowed in the kitchen: 'Your job is to write plays and mine is to keep house; you mind your business and I'll mind mine,' she told him.

The villagers called her the Dragon, which she took as a compliment. She bought a green dragon brooch and told Mr Shaw he was her St George. She dealt swiftly with unwanted phone calls and only allowed callers by appointment. 'If I didn't have Mrs Laden I'd have an Alsatian watchdog,' he told visitors.

My leave over, it was time to go back to London. I don't know how much longer I could have lasted under all the strain, but at the time it seemed that I would have to, because I had been told at the start that this posting would last for at least a year.

By this time I was needing new khaki stockings and other bits of uniform, but whenever I had pleaded to have worn out articles replaced I was told to make them last a little longer. Then, out of the blue, a special order came through that Private Pond could have any new items of uniform she requested. Whatever could be the reason for this sudden change of heart and for the rather odd looks that the officers seemed to be giving me? I had no idea, and it was some time before I unravelled the mystery and got to the bottom of it all.

DESTINATION UNKNOWN

*I*t was good to be able to order any new items of uniform I was needing and have them issued, but I felt sure that there was more to this change in the rules than they were letting on. And I was right. Soon after, I was told to report to an army base at Watford, a few miles north of London.

When I arrived I was summoned to appear before the officer. She looked up and asked 'Name?' in a brisk voice.

I could see all the papers about me in front of her and wondered why I had to answer such an unnecessary question, but I duly told her.

Then she said, 'Who did you work for before you joined the army?'

Again I knew that she had the answer staring her in the face, and by now I was feeling a bit nettled by her manner so I replied, 'A gentleman.'

'I know that,' she said irritably, 'but *who*?'

So I had to tell her, 'Mr Bernard Shaw' – and this satisfied her.

I suppose she was checking that I really was the person they wanted. Then she told me when and where I was to report for further instructions.

It was dark when the time came, and an army car, with a corporal at the wheel, was waiting to take me to my new posting. We were accompanied by an officer. I had no idea where we were going, not then and not even later when we finally arrived. Nothing was said, and it was not for me to ask questions.

It's difficult for people now to realise how secret everything was in wartime. It was hard to tell where you were because sign-posts had been taken away and the names of towns and main railway stations covered over. If you asked someone the way, they weren't supposed to tell you. This was in case enemy spies should parachute down or a large-scale invasion take place. Government posters warned us not to aid the enemy. At night the blackout made things ten times worse. Cars were only allowed to have dim, shaded lights and most places had no street lighting. It was light when there was a full moon, but then again, that was a very mixed blessing because bright moonlight could help enemy planes find their targets.

Once we'd left the town we were soon out in the country, and by the faint lights from the car I could make out the shape of hedgerows ahead of us. We seemed to be travelling mile after mile along narrow country lanes. I'd had no idea that there were so many lanes and hedges in England – not in one stretch. The whole experience seemed more like a dream, and I really did pinch myself once or twice to make sure this was actually happening to me.

At long last we turned in at some gates, and I ventured to ask, 'So is this the beginning of the end?' and a curt 'Yes,' was the only reply I was given. We continued up a long drive, and at last the car came to a halt outside what turned out to be the kitchen quarters of a large house.

The door was opened to let us in. When the lights were switched on again, I was dazzled at first by the sudden brightness. Then I made out the diminutive figure of one of the cooks. (Her name was Doris.) She was holding a pie in one hand and trimming it round with a knife, *and* with her fingers and thumb. 'Mrs Higgs would never have allowed that,' I thought, but I stepped forward to shake her hand, to the surprise of the army officer, who soon took me on into the messroom and introduced me to the rest of the girls. This room would have been the servants' hall in pre-war days.

The girls seemed to be watching me all the time, in a nice, concerned way – even later when I was unpacking my kit-bag. It had been carried upstairs to the bedroom I was to share with three others.

Afterwards, when I'd got to know them better, I asked them why they had been so kind to me when I arrived – which they really were. They said, 'If you could have seen yourself when you first came, you looked so tired and ill.' They certainly looked healthy and rosy-cheeked. Of course, they had been living in the country with good food and none of the bombing we'd had to put up with night and day in London.

There was a guards' camp near the house, and the guardsmen used to do the chauffeuring and carry the coals and do other odd jobs. During that first evening one of the guards came in and asked 'Like some sandwiches, girls?'

There was a chorus of 'Oh yes please, we'd love some sandwiches!'

I was amazed. Wherever was I – somewhere where sandwiches could appear out of the blue? The next thing I knew, a plate of cheese and pickle sandwiches was brought to us. I hadn't seen anything like it for ages. (Food was pretty scarce and cheese was rationed.)

CHEQUERS

In 1910, Arthur Lee, politician and peer, moved into Chequers with his American wife, Ruth, and began to renovate the old house in the beautiful Buckinghamshire countryside. During World War I, it was converted into a military hospital, but in 1921, with great generosity, the Lees gave Chequers to the nation as a country retreat for the Prime Minister's use.

During World War II, Winston Churchill used the house at weekends and invited all kinds of important visitors to stay, to discuss war strategy. Because it was difficult in wartime to get enough staff to do all the work involved, the women's army (ATS) and air force (WAAF) took turns in staffing Chequers, which is why Violet, with her training and experience, was stationed there.

That first weekend Mr Churchill was away, which meant that we were free and I had time to settle in and draw breath. The place was staffed entirely by service people (except for the curator, Mrs Hill). There were four people working in the kitchen, four in the house, four in the dining-room and a sewing-maid – all army personnel. The three services took it in turn for a spell of duty of three years each. At this time it was the Army's turn for duty.

Much later I discovered what lay behind my coming to Chequers. It seems that before I came, some of the ATS girls stationed at Chequers had gone out in an army truck, and there had been an accident. I never heard exactly what happened, and it was never referred to again, but it meant that they needed some replacements. I was tickled when they told me that the call had gone out for some 'out of the ordinary girls'.

'And how did you discover me?' I asked.

'Oh, we saw a letter that had been posted to you from Ayot,' was the answer.

So a bit of detective work lay behind my posting to Chequers. There is no doubt that the fact that I had worked for Mr and Mrs Shaw told in my favour. They realised that I was used to waiting at table and looking after important and well-known people and that I knew how to be discreet.

The other girls enjoyed introducing me to this new world and on the Saturday afternoon of that first free weekend they

Chequers

took me into Princes Risborough, a small town nearby. We went to the Green Café, which soon became a favourite venue. We would sit round the table and order a plate of cakes with our pot of tea. Because it was wartime there would only be a few nice ones among them, so we used to cut all the cakes in half and share them out as fairly as we could.

On that first visit I caught sight of a notice on the café wall about a musical evening at Risborough Baptist Church. (I later found out that the minister, Mr Benskin, his son and the organist too, were very keen on music.) I told the girls that I'd like to go to the Baptist church when I was off duty on a Sunday.

That first Sunday I *was* free, so off I went. The Army Scripture Reader for the area was at the service too, and he asked me to come to the front and talk about becoming a Christian. So I did.

The organist told me months later that during the service he was sure God was saying to him, 'That girl needs somewhere to go.' And for all the time I was at Chequers, he and his wife made their home a second home for me. It was great to have friends to go to when I was off duty as well as a church where I felt at home.

The other girls complained that although they had been stationed there much longer than me, no one had ever asked them out to tea. I said they would get invited out if they went to church. But they weren't prepared to do that. I think they had a strange idea of what my Christian faith was all about. They would say, 'Oh, Violet, you should come to see this film – you'd like it!' And it turned out that it was because there was a vicar in it!

I was given permission, when no one was about, to play the piano at Chequers. It was a grand piano, situated in the Great Hall, but I just used to play the simple hymn tunes I knew and loved.

Then one day some of the other girls told me, 'There's somebody like you down in the kitchen,' and I soon discovered what they meant. While I was playing a hymn this same girl came into the room and started singing along with me. We soon got talking. Her name was Jean, and we became firm friends. We used to say that we met over *Golden Bells*, which was the name of the popular hymn book we both knew and loved.

I started by serving, or waiting at table, 'around the corner' as we used to call it. It was the place where the curator, Mrs Hill, and the secretary had their meals. I must have suited because when some of the girls were demobbed, I was promoted to serve in the dining-room. Then I was made up to sergeant and put in charge of the dining-room work.

WEEKEND ROUTINE AT CHEQUERS

In her book *Clementine Churchill*, Lady Mary Soames (Churchill's daughter) writes: 'Chequers was large enough to accommodate in comfort a skeleton Private Office, two or three telephone operators, the detectives, chauffeurs and despatch riders, as well as family members and up to eight guests. Quite soon the pattern for the weekends took shape: there was nearly always a nucleus of the family, and occasionally a close friend or two, and superimposed on these intimates would be a succession of service chiefs, Cabinet colleagues or specialists in various subjects, who were bidden to "dine and sleep".

'Since all weekends were, as far as Winston was concerned, working days, most guests were invited on a business basis, and it was rare for wives to be included. Many an overworked general, civil servant or Government colleague was reft away from a weekend in the bosom of his own family, to spend perhaps a gruelling twenty-four hours at Chequers. Nevertheless, their sacrifice was not in vain, for it would be quite impossible to overestimate the value of these working weekends, which often resulted in far-reaching and vital decisions, or in a closer understanding between Churchill and those in whose minds and hands lay the waging of the war. Chequers was also invaluable for entertaining important guests from overseas, who particularly appreciated the country-house atmosphere and the lovely surrounding countryside.'

Chequers, like Ayot in the early days, was a weekend house. But there was plenty to be done during the week. We wore our army uniform, a khaki skirt and shirt, with a crossover khaki overall when we were cleaning. Polishing the silver was a big item, and we spent a lot of time in the pantry doing nothing but clean. The guardsmen would often come in for a gossip and to clean their boots. They would use hot tongs to burn the old polish off the leather and it was literally spit, then polish – that's how they got them up so bright. (I discovered that they would polish your shoes and clean your brass uniform buttons too, if they liked you.)

Mrs Churchill

'The uncertainties of my early life', is how Clementine Churchill referred to her troubled childhood and youth. Her mother, Lady Blanche Hozier, was a daughter of the Earl of Airlie, but in spite of aristocratic birth, times were hard for Lady Hozier's children. Their mother was a life-long gambler and was said to have had nine lovers. Much later Mrs Churchill was to have serious doubts about her own parentage, never knowing the true identity of her father. When Clementine was only five years old, her parents separated and mother and children lived in a series of rented rooms.

Clementine was studious and clever but thoughts of university were quickly dismissed by her mother. There was never money for clothes or the hectic social life of other upper class girls, but an aunt bought her a first ball gown and escorted her to other girls' balls, where Clementine's grave beauty brought her admirers as well as proposals of marriage.

It was at a summer ball in 1904 that Winston Churchill first saw Clementine Hozier and was struck by her beauty. She was nineteen, and he was thirty and already a colourful public figure. Four years later they met again, and Churchill fell in love with her on the grand scale. 'Your sweetness and beauty have cast a glory upon my life,' he wrote. The love was mutual and endured Churchill's periods of depression and banishment to the political wilderness as well as the years of success and acclaim. In a marriage lasting fifty-seven years, Clementine was Winston's anchor. For her – as her daughter remembers well – he always came first, second and third.

Churchill

When it was the right season, we'd go down to the kitchen and give a hand shelling peas and topping and tailing gooseberries. When it was fine we would sit out in the courtyard – a kind of quadrangle that the house was built around. (I still dream about that courtyard but in my dreams it's always full of china – I can't think why.) In the colder weather we'd go down to the kitchen with our tin mugs when they were cooking peas or broccoli and bale out some of the water to drink, which was a real treat.

Another of our weekday jobs was to see to the switchboard. Chequers had a special telephone room, and at the weekends the Prime Minister's own telephonists would come down to see to it. But the rest of the time it was mainly the job of the parlour and dining-room girls. The first thing was to learn how to operate the switchboard and then it was a matter of dashing to the phone whenever it rang. When I had learned the ropes I had to teach the other girls how to work the switchboard.

One of them was called Cathy and one day when she had answered the phone she came dashing out in great distress to find me, calling out, 'Violet, Violet, do come quickly – I don't know what he's saying!'

So I hurried to the phone, and when I said, 'Hello!' a man's voice answered, 'I'm speaking from the King George V Hotel in Paris. Would you please tell me how it's coming through.'

I said, 'It's just as if you were in the room.'

'Oh, that's all right,' he said, 'thank you very much.'

Poor Cathy couldn't believe her ears – all the way from France! Of course, nobody would be surprised these days, but a call from abroad just after the war was something then. Fortunately I took it in my stride.

Another girl I had to teach was Elsie – poor Elsie, always rushing around with a handkerchief to her runny nose. She really hadn't a clue but she was such a dear, and we got on well and somehow I had to teach her to use this switchboard.

There was a funny sequel to that. Elsie was demobbed before me, and one day she rang me up. 'I had to ring,' she said, 'guess what? I'm a telephonist. And I want to thank you

Mr Churchill with Mrs Churchill

for teaching me how to use the switchboard because that's how I got the job.' I think it was a step up for her because before she joined up she had been living in Camberwell, working in a lampshade factory.

It's open countryside all around Chequers, and naturally security was tight – though nothing like it would be these days. At night time army police would check that all the windows were properly fastened and watchmen would patrol the grounds. Every day we would be given a bit of paper with the password for the day written on it, and unless we could give the password we wouldn't be allowed in or out of the grounds. But if you got stuck you went to the guards' camp, where they knew you.

One of my funnier moments at Chequers, though it wasn't funny at the time, was when there was a fire drill. We were all told beforehand that it was to happen, but no one told us what we had to do when the alarm went. So when the fire bell sounded, we all acted in a rather haphazard way.

The fire officer came up to me, and I said my piece, that I felt we hadn't been given proper instructions.

So he asked me, 'Well, what *would* you do if there was a fire?'

I said, 'I'd get out quick!'

But it turned out that what I should have done was to pick up a Queen Anne chair and rescue it at the same time, so that we would save as many treasures from the house as possible as well as saving our own lives.

At one practice Mrs Hill and I watched the guards rolling barrels of water up to the house. Mrs Hill said, 'Violet, the house would have burned down before help arrived!'

Fire-fighting methods improved later, and fortunately there was never a fire nor an air-raid either, although there were plenty of air-raid practices too. The guards were in charge and we would hear trucks lumbering up to the doors ready to save the house.

THE PRISON ROOM AT CHEQUERS

A strange marriage indeed – held at night by candle-light in the bridegroom's sparse apartments in West-minster. He was middle-aged, powerful – seven foot tall in his stocking feet – and his bride was a tiny, freckled, red-head still in her teens. But more than physical dif-ferences separated the two. The bridegroom, Thomas Keyes, was an untitled servant of the Queen – a ser-geant porter and a widower with several children – and his young bride, Mary Grey, was a princess of royal blood, a great-granddaughter of King Henry VII.

In 1553 her older sister, Lady Jane, had been pro-claimed Queen for nine days, before Mary Tudor ascended the throne. Jane was dispatched to the Tower of London and later beheaded. Now, five years later, when Elizabeth I had succeeded her half-sister as Queen, Lady Mary Grey took her life in her hands when she married without the queen's consent and chose a bridegroom quite outside court circles.

News of the secret wedding was quickly relayed to Queen Elizabeth, and Keyes and his children were sent to the notorious Fleet Prison. But what was to be done with the unfortunate princess? As a claimant to the throne she must be closely guarded so Elizabeth ban-ished her to Chequers, the home of wealthy business-man Sir William Hawtrey, with instructions for her strict confinement.

Mary rode from London with Sir William, only her maid and a groom in attendance. Mud-stained, exhausted and weeping, she climbed the stairs into the attic room, which was to be her home for two years. The Prison Room, as it is now called, is twelve- foot square, with stone walls. On one of these walls a glass panel protects the original inscription carved by Lady Mary, which no one has ever deciphered. Violet tells how the staff on duty at that end of the house avoided those stairs and that room whenever they could. They believed that it was haunted.

Chequers is beautiful, and the house goes back a long way. There is a secret room reached by a secret stairway where Lady Mary Grey was kept prisoner in Tudor times. The girls were not keen on going to that part of the house because it was supposed to be haunted, but in my time it was mainly used by Mr Churchill's grandchildren (the Sandys family) and their nanny.

Of course we weren't there to enjoy the house or stroll round the garden. We didn't see much more of the house than the rooms where we were on duty. And when we went into those rooms we were kept busy all the time, cleaning or cooking, or, in my case, waiting at table.

But with all the important guests who came to Chequers, my job, you may guess, had its very interesting side – as I soon discovered.

7

THE PRIME MINISTER AT HOME

The first sign that the Prime Minister was coming to Chequers was the arrival of the police. They were always sent ahead to check out the place.

We asked no questions, and we were never informed in so many words, but we knew well enough when it was going to be 'action stations'. If important visitors had been invited, the police would check the guest rooms too.

Of course, definite news must have filtered through somehow because Mrs Hill always knew how many were coming. Chequers Home Farm provided fresh food, and Mrs Hill would go into Aylesbury on the Friday to get what other provisions were needed. It might depend on what visitors were expected. For example we had to have oranges and grapefruit for General Montgomery whenever he came. He didn't drink alcohol at all.

FIELD MARSHAL BERNARD MONTGOMERY

Monty – as he was affectionately known – will always be remembered for the key allied victory that he won at

El Alamein. He took over the North Africa campaign following bitter allied defeat and heartened his troops by his own enthusiasm and charisma. Refusing to live in the luxurious house assigned as his command base, he camped instead in a caravan in the grounds. Although he was strictly teetotal and non-smoking himself, he made sure that his men had the cigarettes they craved.

Montgomery was less popular with the officers and the powers-that-be, who considered him arrogant and pompous. He returned to Britain, following his victory at El Alamein, to make a morale-boosting tour of munitions factories, and Churchill grew fed up with his self-importance. At Churchill's weekly audience at the Palace, he told King George VI, 'I'm a bit worried about Monty; I think he's after my job.' 'Thank goodness,' the King replied, 'I thought he was after mine.'

Lieutenant Colonel John Kimmins remembers Monty's visit to the Military Academy at Sandhurst long after the war. He arrived resplendent in his 'Number One' dress and began by telling the cadets: 'When I was at Sandhurst, my Instructor said I was useless . . . [pregnant pause] – and *he* ended up a major.' That brought the house down. Only the senior instructors present were not amused.

There would usually be about fourteen for dinner at weekends, and Mrs Hill would arrange the seating and do the place names for the dinner table.

It was a lovely room and although food was none too plentiful or elaborate in wartime, it was always beautifully served.

They'd start with a soup, then slices of meat arranged on a large silver salver, with plenty of nice fresh vegetables to accompany it. This would be followed by a sweet, which was usually a fruit fool, say damson, because there were lots of vegetables and fruit from the gardens. There would be a lovely bowl of fresh fruit too. They'd end with a savoury which was usually tiny little bits of toast with something on, hardly worth collecting a plateful I thought, but they seemed to like it. It was a pleasure to serve there, and I really enjoyed the whole refined atmosphere at Chequers.

As time went by, the girls who came to replace the ones being demobbed weren't used to waiting at table and not very interested in doing it, so that made a lot of extra work for me. But Cathy was good, and she would stay on to help me with all the clearing up. She was older than I was, and I really appreciated her helping me like that, and I told her so. She just said, 'Violet, I was in hotel work and you were in private work – there is a difference.' I thought of that when I saw a programme on television about living below stairs in an Edwardian house. The chef just banged the plates down so quickly that I knew he must have been in hotel work. In a private house you handled each plate very gently, because it was precious family china.

My biggest worry was the wines. Mrs Higgs had trained me in everything else but no wine was drunk at Ayot. Mr Shaw was strictly teetotal, and alcohol was never served. I didn't know anything about wine, and unfortunately the bottles don't come with instructions, in fact they didn't even give the names in English! Of course during the war there weren't the huge number of different wines to choose from that there are today, but I was still unsure of myself. I used to wonder whatever I should do. But God was good to me and helped me, and I survived. Aiming straight with the soda siphon was a problem at first but I soon found a way around that. I used to take the glass to the sideboard and squirt the soda in without an audience watching, and me ruining the cloth.

PEARL HARBOUR

On 7 December 1941, the Japanese bombed the American naval base of Pearl Harbour. Churchill was dining with two Americans – Averell Harriman, an old friend of his, and John Winant, the American ambassador to Britain. Churchill turned on his wireless at the table to hear the nine o'clock news, but reception was not clear. At that moment Mr Sawyers, the butler, came bursting into the dining-room. He had been listening to the wireless in the pantry and came to announce the startling news. Churchill and his two friends leaped from the table and rushed to the telephone to talk to President Roosevelt. 'What's this about Japan?' Churchill thundered down the line. 'It's true,' Roosevelt replied, 'they've attacked us at Pearl Harbour. We are all in the same boat now.'

When Mr Churchill was there, all the guests would go up with him after dinner to see a film. That was our opportunity to valet their day clothes. We would brush and press the suits and take them to the appropriate rooms. When I was valeting for any of the gentlemen that was my job and I had to lay out their evening clothes in advance as well, with a clean handkerchief ready on the chair. In the morning it was a matter of asking what they wanted to wear that day when you took them their morning tea. I'd sometimes have to draw the bath for them too (I've done that for Mr Churchill).

All these things I had to learn the hard way and with much prayer for God's help. I had to pick up how to do these things as I went along. But there were never any complaints so that must mean that I can't have gone too far wrong.

Mr Churchill always brought Mr Sawyers with him, he was his own butler-valet. He was quite a character, but we got on well together in a quiet way. He found out that I missed going to church, because there was no weekend leave when the Prime Minister was there, and so he used to switch on the hymn-singing programme on the wireless so that I could hear it. I thought it was very considerate of him.

Sometimes he'd be in the kitchen and there'd be a 'ping' from one of the room bells, and we all knew it was Mr Churchill's bell being rung. Soon after there'd be another 'ping', and Mr Sawyers would mutter, 'I'm coming, I'm coming!' By the time the bell had rung for the third time Mr Sawyers would be on his way up the stairs. Suspended from his collar was a coat hanger with Mr Churchill's clothes on it, and in one hand he carried a tray while under the other arm was Mr Churchill's cat. It was a sight to behold I can tell you. It was a black cat.

WINSTON CHURCHILL'S CAT

Nelson – so-called because Churchill had rescued the cat when he was First Lord at the Admiralty – accompanied his master to Number 10 when he became Prime Minister. He was soon more than a match for the resident Downing Street cat, named Treasury Bill. Nelson liked to sit on a chair beside Churchill while he was working, but he was afraid of the noise of the anti-aircraft gunfire. 'Try to remember what those boys in the RAF are doing,' Churchill used to tell him. So Nelson was evacuated to Chequers. At weekends he would sleep on Churchill's bed, curled up on the Prime Minister's feet. Churchill used to tell people that his cat was doing more to help the war effort than they were. By keeping his feet warm Nelson saved the fuel that would have been used to boil a kettle for a hot water bottle.

Most guests took breakfast in bed so we laid up the trays in the pantry the night before. There was quite an army of trays to prepare. First we'd put a tray cloth, then china, cutlery and toast rack. Next morning the first job was to take morning tea to the guests. It wasn't unknown in the rush and bustle to send up a pot of tea without the tea in it, just hot water. I'll admit I've done it myself. But everyone was very good-natured and easy-going. We'd draw back the bedroom curtains, but then it was for the housemaids to take them their shaving water in big copper jugs.

Our next job was to complete the breakfast trays. It was not a lavish breakfast like it would be now. (Cooked breakfast was served in the dining-room for those who wanted it.) There'd be a half grapefruit, ready prepared, cereal and toast. The marmalade would be put out in a jam pot, and the butter made into individual 'roundies' and arranged on a glass dish. Then there would be the teapot, hot water jug and milk jug of course.

The upstairs staff were responsible for the bedroom fires, but we had to see to those in the Great Hall, the dining-room and the study. These were the downstairs rooms where most things went on. The guards at the camp used to line up buckets full of coal and logs in the courtyard for us, and they would often bring them inside to help us, but if no one was around we had to carry them in ourselves. It took a whole bucket of coal for each fireplace.

Eisenhower

Of course, we had our favourite guests, as well as those we weren't so happy with. Some of the regular visitors from abroad, especially the Americans, would whisper in our ear at dinner to inquire about any girls that were absent. They'd remember their names and ask if one or another was all right and send a kind message. That meant a lot to us. General Eisenhower was another great favourite.

DWIGHT EISENHOWER

Ike – as he was known – was the third of six boys born to hard-working, God-fearing parents in Abilene, Texas. Bible-reading and family prayers were a regular part of the day's routine. Their parents encouraged the boys, in true American style, to take every opportunity that life offered. Eisenhower put heart and soul into all he did, and although he hated war, he was the conquering hero in the Allied invasion of World War II and also a United States president who secured eight years of peace.

Sir Stafford and Lady Cripps, both very tall people, were frequent visitors. Lady Cripps always liked a second cup of coffee and was very pleased that we tried to remember that.

SIR STAFFORD CRIPPS

'There but for the grace of God goes – God!' Churchill once remarked of Sir Stafford Cripps. Cripps was a Christian Socialist (a nephew of Beatrice Webb) and a devout practising Christian who lived by his principles. In World War I he served with the Red Cross because he was a pacifist, and although he later made a lot of money as a barrister, he lived simply and gave his money to the Socialist cause.

During World War II, Cripps was Churchill's chief critic, so Churchill shrewdly decided to make him a member of his War Cabinet. Cripps was a vegetarian and neither smoked nor drank. Harold Nicholson wrote in his diary that Cripps 'would find the atmosphere of Downing Street, with its late hours, casual talk, cigar smoke and endless whisky unpalatable'. He added that Churchill, for his part, 'never regards with affection a man of such inhuman austerity as Cripps'. After a short while, Cripps was downgraded; he left the Cabinet and was put in charge of aircraft production. He took the demotion graciously and put all his energies into his new job.

One charming visitor was General Smuts, the South African Prime Minister. Usually a guardsman would carry the bags in when a car drew up, but there was no one around to help the day he arrived. So when I went to the door and let General Smuts in, I picked up his bags and humped them up the stairs to his bedroom myself. By the time he arrived I was on my hands and knees unpacking for him.

Smuts

JAN SMUTS

As the second son in his family, Jan Smuts, born in 1870, was destined to work on the family farm. His father said that Jan was a 'poor, unhealthy youngster... without much intelligence'. He could not have been more mistaken. When the first-born son died, Jan, now twelve, took his place. He was sent to school and proved to be a brilliant student. He won a scholarship at Cambridge University, where he took prize after prize. As well as being a brilliant scientist he had a great love of poetry and literature as well as philosophy and botany. Smuts refused a professorship at Cambridge and returned to South Africa where he twice became Prime Minister. He and Churchill developed a deep friendship that lasted almost fifty years, and Smuts was one of the few people Churchill would listen to. Churchill declared, 'My faith in Smuts is unbreakable. He is a great man.'

He said, 'My dear young lady, you should never carry bags like that. Don't worry, my aide will do it all.' His aide was a very handsome young man, and he was waiting there ready to take over from me. And guess who he was? General Smuts' own son!

I used to do the unpacking for all the Commonwealth Prime Ministers who visited Chequers. Mostly they arrived with big leather cases that had fitted compartments. So unpacking and packing again for them when they were leaving was quite a straightforward job. I was specially pleased when I found a Bible tucked among all their other belongings. I'd put it ready for them to read, on the table beside the bed.

John Winant

I've said how friendly the American visitors were but I could scarcely believe what happened to me one evening. Mr Winant, the American Ambassador to Britain, was at Chequers, and his chauffeur, Mr Norberry, was in the kitchen with the rest of us and with some of the staff belonging to other guests.

I was talking about how I was hoping to get up to London. We usually caught a train at Wendover station but I still needed a lift to the station.

To my amazement Mr Norberry said cheerily, 'My boss will take you, we're going back to London soon.'

I was shocked at such a suggestion, but no sooner said than done. Mr Norberry went off to speak to the ambassador and came back saying, 'That's okay – he'll give you a lift.'

JOHN GILBERT ('GIL') WINANT

Kindness characterised John Winant's career. Moved by the novels of Charles Dickens, he felt deeply the need to right injustices and prevent cruelty. When President Roosevelt appointed him head of the new Social Security Board, Winant approached the work with a genuine desire to help the underprivileged and bring about change.

During the difficult days of World War II Roosevelt appointed him ambassador to Britain. Instead of living in the grand and stately ambassador's residence, however, he opted for modest apartments next door and subsisted on the same restricted rations as ordinary Londoners. After a night of bombing, he would walk the streets bringing comfort wherever he could – a symbol of strength and hope in the darkest days. The British public loved him and were strengthened and cheered by his genuine kindness and compassion.

When Winant resigned his office in 1946, Churchill held a special celebration for him at Mansion House. He said of Winant: 'He is a friend of Britain, but more than a friend of Britain – he is a friend of justice, freedom and truth.'

I was horrified at the thought of travelling with the ambassador. 'Where shall I sit?' I asked Mr Norberry.

He said, 'He'll tell you.'

When Mr Winant was ready to leave, I asked timidly, 'Where shall I sit?'

He replied, 'In the back with me.'

I have to admit that I sat on the edge of the seat and didn't really make the most of the luxury travel.

I couldn't think of a thing to say but at last I plucked up courage and asked, 'What are places like in America?'

Mr Winant just gestured out of the window at the approaches to London and answered, 'Much like that.'

It did get quite exciting as we got nearer to London and the car had to slow down for traffic. People gazed in wonder at the large limousine and peered curiously at us inside.

The chauffeur stopped at Claridge's Hotel for Mr Winant to get out, but before he left he said to Mr Norberry, 'Take Violet wherever she wants to go.'

You can be sure I enjoyed that last bit of the journey and turned up at my destination in full splendour.

I was not one for London really, and apart from occasional visits I was happy to be stationed at Chequers in the heart of the country, yet still able to feel so near the centre of all that was happening in the nation.

But although I didn't know it then, it would soon be London for me, whether I liked it or not.

C 8 D

SUMMONED TO NUMBER 10

*I*n May 1945, the war in Europe was over and the celebrations had begun. But it was to be a long time before everything returned to normal. Of course lots of young people couldn't even remember much about a time before there was a war, and most of us had forgotten what normal life was like anyway.

We weren't all demobbed at once from the Army – and food shortages and rationing didn't end for a very long time. But life for me, serving in the army at Chequers, looked as if it would continue for a while uninterrupted.

Then a rumour went round that one of the girls who waited at table at Number 10 Downing Street had gone sick. This of course is the Prime Minister's official residence in London and his main base of operations. Any vacancies there were top priority to be filled so we guessed that someone experienced would be sent from Chequers to stand in for her. I wasn't next in order for such a promotion; one or two girls had been at Chequers longer than I had. But out of the blue I got my orders to go to Number 10. It turned out that Mr Sawyers, Mr Churchill's butler-valet, had asked for me particularly, so I jumped the queue, but it was not my doing. I

Number 10 Downing Street

suppose that once again it was my training under Mrs Higgs that stood me in good stead. So I packed up to go and was told that I would be met when I arrived in London.

A car took me to Wendover railway station where I caught the train. When I arrived at Baker Street another army car was waiting to drive me to Downing Street. It was a very exciting time for the whole country, with the war in Europe just ended, and London was at the very centre of all the rejoicing. In fact as we drove along through London we found some of the roads already closed in preparation for the Thanksgiving Service which was to take place in Westminster Abbey. It felt good to be waved through streets that had been cordoned off from all the usual traffic, because we were on the Prime Minister's business.

THANKSGIVING SERVICE AT ST PAUL'S CATHEDRAL

Several times during the war, the Government declared special Days of National Prayer. On 13 May 1945, King George VI led the thanksgiving at a service in St Paul's Cathedral at which politicians and dignitaries were present. Places in the cathedral were also reserved for fifty housewives representing ordinary people whose efforts had also helped to win the war.

'Chips' (Sir Henry) Channon, an American expatriate, wrote in his diary: 'I went to St Paul's for the great Thanksgiving Service, very hot in my morning clothes. The great cathedral was crowded, and I watched all the notabilities of the earth come in, and listened to the cheers of the crowd outside.' But there was poignancy as memories of the tragedy of war were symbolised by the temporary altar and the bomb-damaged choir, where the RAF orchestra played. The death toll in the war numbered 400,000 military and 65,000 civilian men, women and children.

When we had almost reached Downing Street the driver told me to get out of the car and stand on the running-board. I did as I was told – I hadn't been in the Army for nothing – and was just in time to see the Royal Family go past the bottom of the street in an open carriage. There were the two Princesses – Princess Elizabeth, as our Queen was then – and her younger sister Princess Margaret. They were both dressed in a yellow-gold colour which gleamed in the light. It all looked so beautiful, a sight I'll never forget.

10 DOWNING STREET

Ten Downing Street is the best-known address in England. *Number 10* identifies the Prime Minister's house, even though the nameplate *First Lord of the Treasury* is engraved on the front door. That was the post held by Sir Robert Walpole, who lived there from 1721 to 1742 and was Britain's first Prime Minister in all but name. When Number 10 was offered to him as a personal gift, Walpole would not accept it for himself but as the future home for First Lords. The title *Prime Minister* is used now, but the title on the door is unchanged.

The house is bigger than it looks from outside, consisting of two houses joined together, one fronting Downing Street and the other behind it, overlooking Horse Guards Parade. Since World War I, a policeman has been permanently stationed outside the front door, and an attendant waits just inside to let visitors or residents in and out. Not even the Prime Minister has a key.

The Cabinet Room, where the cabinet meets on Thursdays, is separated from the rest of the building by soundproofed double doors. Ministers sit around a boat-shaped table, and the Prime Minister sits with his back to the fireplace in the only chair with arms. If he is not present, his chair is left at an angle so that he can return quickly.

Along the splendid staircase (which Violet did *not* use) hang portraits of all the previous Prime Ministers. When a Prime Minister leaves office, his or her photograph is added, and each portrait moves down one place.

The state rooms are on the first floor. They are used for meetings with heads of state and for television interviews. Since the 1930s, the Prime Minister and his family have been consigned to living in a flat 'over the shop'.

When we arrived at Number 10 the door was opened for us. The door was not operated electronically; there is always someone there in person waiting to let visitors in.

I was shown to my room, but of course we didn't use the splendid main staircase that is often shown on television. We had to sheer off to the right after we got inside the front door and go up the back way. The servants' bedrooms had all been recently refurbished and were really nice. I was delighted with my room.

Everyone was so courteous and polite, and the detectives were specially helpful. The ones most often on duty while I was there were Inspector Hughes and Sergeant Green. They seemed to have the knack of knowing just when we all needed to be jollied along and when it was best to leave us alone to get on with it. They were always so nice and understanding, they realised what a hectic time it was for us.

MRS CHURCHILL AND THE RED CROSS IN RUSSIA

In 1942, just after Mrs Churchill launched the Aid to Russia Fund with the Red Cross, money began pouring in. Britain was aware of how much was owed to the Russian involvement in the war and how deeply the ordinary people were suffering. But meeting the needs of this vast country was like trying to fill a bottomless pit. Mrs Maisky, the wife of the Russian Ambassador Ivan Maisky, was Mrs Churchill's main contact at the Embassy in London. Dealing with Mrs Maisky called for much patience and tact. She always had a long list of requests to make as well as complaints.

But Mrs Churchill's work *was* appreciated, and in 1945 she was invited to visit Russia to see how the funds had been used. The highlight of her visit was a meeting with Stalin; Mrs Churchill handed him the gift of a gold fountain pen from Mr Churchill and said, 'My husband wished me to express the hope that you will write him many friendly messages with it.' Stalin took the pen with a smile; then, putting it to one side, he said, 'But I only write in pencil.'

You can imagine that I was a bit nervous about serving that first meal. Mrs Churchill was in Russia with the Red Cross at the time, but one of their daughters, Mary, was at home. She was in the Army too. There were other visitors, but lunch was served informally at a round table in the drawing-room. That made serving much more tricky, as I was trying to avoid unexpected chair and table legs.

MARY CHURCHILL (LADY SOAMES)

Mary, the Churchill's youngest child, joined the ATS when she was eighteen and stayed for five years, first in the ranks and later as an officer with anti-aircraft batteries.

In later life she said, 'It was the biggest experience of my life. I was catapulted out of my narrow class background and I was independent. . . . Uniform is a tremendous leveller.' But being posted to a new unit was an ordeal: 'I knew they'd be saying: "Here's Churchill's daughter – she won't be scrubbing any floors!" You had to start all over again and make the point that you weren't just there to polish your nails. It was much easier when I was in the ranks. Once you were an officer, it was far more of a struggle to be accepted. I remember my terror whenever I was sent to a new unit' (as quoted in the *Daily Telegraph*, 16 August 2002).

I thought I was serving as discreetly as I could when I realised with amazement that Mr Churchill was addressing *me* – and in front of everyone. 'I hear you have come from Chequers to help us,' he said.

'Yes, sir,' I replied.

Then he turned to his daughter, 'Mary, get up and help the young lady,' by which he meant her to move her place to make things easier for me to do the serving. And without another word she did. It certainly was a help but I was full of confusion to think that she, a captain, had been ordered to move for me, a mere private at that time. But that was the whole attitude and atmosphere at Number 10 when Mr Churchill was there.

When dinner was served in the dining-room it was much easier for us because the room and furniture were designed for the purpose. There weren't as many to serve as at Chequers, say eight to ten at the most, but even so there was a lot for us to do.

At Number 10, there was only Mr Sawyers and me to do all the waiting and serving between us. I can't remember if we ever had anyone else helping; it was a very small staff. I expect they would have called in extra help from the barracks for a really big occasion.

It was very exciting being at Downing Street. I'd lie in bed at night and hear Big Ben boom out the hours, and I'd think to myself, 'It's all happening here – and I'm here too.' I felt very privileged.

But it was also exhausting, and there was a lot of work to do. In the mornings there was the silver to clean. At Chequers, right in the country, we did the silver once a week, but here in London we had to clean it all every single day – and there was a lot of it.

During the afternoon Mr Sawyers would say, 'Go out and get some air in the park before getting ready for the evening work.'

I enjoyed mingling with the crowds who were always milling around, hoping they'd catch sight of someone important. In the evening, while we were serving dinner, we could hear the crowds outside chanting over and over, 'We want Churchill! We want Churchill!' and I'd think, Well, you can't – he's having his dinner!'

VE DAY

On 7 May 1945 Germany surrendered, and Churchill declared victory in Europe and a national holiday on 8 May. VE Day was a time of exuberant celebration. Tom Fletcher, then a teenager, describes the scene: 'The whole world seemed to go crazy with dancing, singing and parties in the street and celebration drinks.... The Government announced a Victory Parade would take place in London on 10 August and my future brother-in-law suggested that we should go. We planned to catch the early morning "milk train" to Paddington. During the night I was ferried on the back of his motor-bike to Temple Meads station, and he then returned for my sister. Leaving the bike at the station we caught the 4.00 a.m. milk train.

'On arriving at Paddington we had some directions from a Cockney local who advised, "Go dahn the back streets, mater," and we found our way to Oxford Street. The crowds were already about four deep from the front of the pavement and we found the best spot possible. Standing on tiptoe we witnessed a wonderful, colourful, uplifting procession of marching bands and representatives of all the armed forces. The cheering and flag waving was non-stop.'

It was when I was at Downing Street for VE Day that Mr Sawyers said to me, 'There's somebody very important coming to dinner tonight, so go out and get some air and prepare yourself for this evening.' He said it so seriously, and of course I was bursting with curiosity to know who it was, but it never occurred to me to ask. It's hard to explain these days, but we were used to obeying orders and waiting to be told what we needed to know when the time

Fireworks to celebrate VE Day in London

came. But as I strolled around in the park in the early summer warmth, the big question was in my mind. Who could it be that was expected? And how would I cope with it?

When I arrived back at Number 10, I found to my horror that Mr Sawyers was tipsy. Very reluctantly and dismally he told me, 'Plans have been altered. But there is another important personage coming.'

In the end I learned that it had been the King himself, King George VI, who had been expected for dinner and that was why Mr Sawyers had been so pleased and why he was so disappointed now. He was really keen for me to have the chance to be there when the King came. But my only thought at the time was, 'Well, you wouldn't have been much help to me the way you are now!'

Just in case I ever needed to wait on His Majesty, I asked Mr Sawyers (once he was sober again), 'What would I have to do differently if the King should come?'

And he replied, 'Just keep his place clean' – he meant to brush away any crumbs and so forth. I still wondered if I would have been too nervous if the King had come, but I suppose I would have risen to it.

The important personage who did come to dinner that night was General Eisenhower (later President of the United States). Of course we were used to having him at Chequers, but it was always a treat. I'd be standing there, waiting for the guests to come in, and the whole room would light up when he arrived. He was a lovely, friendly man.

He used to greet us when he came in (not something that Field Marshal Montgomery would ever do) and always knew the names of those of us who waited at table and would look around to see if anyone was missing. I think he and other overseas guests enjoyed coming to Chequers and Number 10.

One of them whispered to me one day, as he sat down at the table, 'It's like coming home.'

It was always high tension at Downing Street for one reason or another. There was very little time for chatting or larking around, though I must admit that when Mr Sawyers and I met at the swing doors, we would sometimes squirt each other with the soda siphon, but only in passing – there was no time to hang around.

One thing I had to get used to was the fact that, at a given signal, everyone and everything had to be moved to the Annexe for security. We never knew when it would happen, but at that signal, a waiting army truck would transport us, the food and all the equipment, and carry everything off to the Annexe. It was a system of underground passages where the Prime Minister could work, eat and sleep in security.

THE CABINET WAR ROOMS

'The most surprising thing is how plain, cramped and democratic the subterranean quarters must have been.... It must have stunk. Everyone smoked, Churchill continuously. There was no air-conditioning, with the air having been forced down tubes that resembled an old ship's ventilation system. There were no flush lavatories.' Michael Binyon imagined what wartime conditions must have been like when he wrote in *The Times* about the new areas of the Cabinet War Rooms opened to the public in 2003. Everything has been done to reconstruct the wartime furnishings – with maps, old-style bakelite telephones and the famous Map Room. To make the reconstruction more realistic there are 'staff' on duty dressed in army uniform and exchanging wartime slang. Violet's opinion is that the whole complex has been considerably smartened up since her day.

It was 1938 when building work began on the 'London underneath London'. The central War Room was opened up on 27 August 1939, and it was then that the map keepers began their first watch in the Map Room; the lights would not be switched off for the next six years. The underground complex contained the all-important Cabinet Room, where Churchill and a select group of ministers and advisers met, and small bedrooms for Mr and Mrs Churchill, as well as a pantry for Mr Sawyers, furnished with only the bare essentials. Linking them all was a maze of criss-crossing passages, which Violet remembers only too well.

We had a kitchen there, but it was pretty basic, although there were the bare essentials. There was a fridge but there was so little space that it had to be put right up against the wall, with no space behind for ventilation. My job was to serve the meals in the dining-room there, but it was very low-key compared with Downing Street, and we didn't have the splendid dishes and silver that we used at Number 10.

One day in the War Cabinet Rooms, I was feeling hopelessly dizzy and confused with all the labyrinth of passages. There I was, holding a tray of tea I was supposed to be taking to someone, and I didn't know which way to go. In my desperation I thought of Mrs Hill, who I had waited on at Chequers and who had now been transferred to London as one of Mr Churchill's private secretaries. There was a phone in the corridor so I picked it up and rang her number. She listened, then said in her lovely ladylike voice, 'Just describe to me where you are.' I was able to do that, and she said, 'Just wait there, and I will send someone down to help you.' And that is exactly what she did.

When my stint at Downing Street ended I would be exhausted. When I got back to Chequers, I was allowed to rest up a bit and take it easy at least until the weekend activity began and visitors arrived. You see, I was only sent to Downing Street when someone was ill or on leave. When that happened, Mrs Hill would phone through to Chequers and the summons would come for me to go post haste to London.

I suppose that nothing in my life has ever been more exciting than those times at Number 10 – especially on VE and VJ Days. I was there on both of those victory days and shall never forget them.

But however exciting it was to be there at the heart of things, and I felt really privileged, my life has been anything but downhill in the days and years that have followed. I've had the most wonderful and varied experiences since then, as you will soon see, sometimes to do with celebrities and the limelight but always with hard work and with true happiness and contentment.

9

ELECTION SHOCK

The war may have been over, but the busy routine at Chequers continued. After a stint at Downing Street, I would sometimes have a few days to let up before it was Friday again and we were all immersed in the usual bustle and preparations for the arrival of the Prime Minister and his guests for the weekend.

But summer 1945 was notable for something more than the end of the war. It was announced that there was to be a general election. Of course, we all thought it was a foregone conclusion that Mr Churchill would be re-elected. He was everyone's hero, and we all knew that it was through him that we had won the war.

Just before the election I was due to go on leave. I was just coming through the pantry door when Mr Sawyers spoke to me. 'This will be your last leave from Chequers, Violet,' he said, 'because you'll be going up to Number 10.'

I suppose I should have been gratified, but instead I felt a surge of panic. 'Oh, no,' I thought, 'I don't think I can do it.' I loved the work and all the excitement of being at Downing Street and felt very privileged to be there, but it was so demanding and such stressful work – and I just wasn't strong enough. How was I going to cope with it?

At that moment a voice inside me said, 'Don't worry, you won't be going.' I'm absolutely sure that was God's voice speaking to me and calming my fears because I never worried about it after that and felt quite peaceful about the future.

Life hadn't been quite the same at Chequers once the war ended. Many of the more experienced girls who were used to the work there were being demobbed now, and the new ones who took their place really weren't interested in the job. They said outright that they hadn't joined the ATS to do work like this, by which they meant housework and cleaning. So standards slipped, and I used to find dust where it had no business to be and even discovered that the Prime Minister's coal scuttle had been left empty. It wasn't really my job anymore, but I used to polish the floorboards on my hands and knees with Mansion polish rather than let them go dirty.

I can remember one morning when Mrs Hill and I were in the Hawtrey Room (a lovely room, which has a cabinet with a few mementoes from the time of Queen Elizabeth I and Cromwell, including Queen Elizabeth's ring). There were a couple of girls over the other side of the room engrossed in doing something, I can't remember what. But they did it the wrong way, and Mrs Hill said to me, 'Oh Violet, what is England coming to if it's going to depend on girls like that!' And there was no answer I could give.

Mrs Hill was a lovely person. She had spent some years with her husband in India, but she used to suffer from bad headaches. So when she wasn't well I used to look after her a bit, and she would say, 'Oh Violet, you should have been a nurse!' (I was often told that. I would have loved to be one, and it wasn't for lack of trying, but perhaps I hadn't the stamina.)

Then came the shock of the election – poor Mr Churchill! He was out and the Labour Government was in.

We were so sad when Mr and Mrs Churchill, together, came to say good-bye to all of us on the staff at Chequers. We lined up in the mess room, and they shook hands with each one of us in turn and thanked us. I felt so sad.

Then, of course, we had the Attlees – the new Prime Minister and his wife.

CLEMENT ATTLEE

Clement Attlee came from a comfortable middle-class background and after public school and Oxford was called to the bar in 1905. But he understood what it meant to be poor, unemployed and living in squalor because he had helped at a boys' club in London's East End. He joined the Fabian Society and the Independent Labour Party and later represented Limehouse, in London's East End, as their Member of Parliament.

As the new Prime Minister, Chequers became Mr Attlee's country home for the next six years, and the staff were in for changes. Mr Attlee dressed formally and wore a stiff shirt and wing collar at dinner, whereas Mr Churchill had relaxed in one of his siren suits, sometimes topped by a colourful silk dressing-gown. Nor were the meals as good because someone from the ATS replaced Mrs Churchill's excellent cook. At least everyone was able to get to bed a good deal earlier than in Churchill's day.

When Churchill became Prime Minister again in 1951 he was anxious not to hustle the Attlees out of

Number 10 and Chequers. He wrote to Mr Attlee: 'My wife and I will not be coming to C for at least a month, so pray use it in any way convenient.' But Chequers was to change hands once again.

Mr Attlee didn't have his own servant so it was my job to valet for him as well as to wait at table. I can't say that I ever remember any kind of conversation with him, nothing whatever – he was a very quiet man. But I do remember one very telling incident.

Mr Attlee was not having an easy time, what with bread rationing and some problem with one of the lady MPs in his cabinet, I think. I happened to catch him sitting with his head in his hands and I thought: This is what the public knows nothing about – the bad days and the constant strain. I never forgot that picture of him.

Christmas was usually a special time at Chequers with families of the Prime Minister arriving, and I can recall one very memorable Christmas during Mr Attlee's time. They gave a party for local children. I don't know how it was all planned, but it was done with military precision. Our part was to see to laying the tables and setting everything out. We made waterlilies out of the serviettes to look pretty. The highlight of the party was when the children lined up and shouted up the chimney, 'We want Father Christmas!' All of a sudden Father Christmas appeared, dressed in his red robe and with a white beard. Of course it was the Prime Minister himself. It was very cleverly done, and there was great excitement all round.

After Mr and Mrs Attlee had gone back to London, the girls who were on duty in Downing Street rang through to us at Chequers and said, 'Whatever did you do with them at

Christmas? They haven't stopped talking about it, they had such a lovely time.' So we felt pleased and surprised too, for it was quite something for them to make so much of it.

I was promoted to corporal and then to sergeant, and I shall always be grateful for the way the girls accepted me. When I was in charge, I did try to keep Sunday respected. The first time on duty on a Sunday, I heard the sound of scrubbing coming from the kitchen. I announced, 'No scrubbing on a Sunday, we have all week for that.' This was quite in order as in other households there would be no rough work done on Sundays. There were always some staff off duty anyway, so work was kept to a minimum.

The other thing I tried to do, without much success, was to keep the girls in at nights. I had a pretty good idea what went on when they did go out.

One evening one of the guards tried to persuade me to go to the Bernard Arms with the rest of the crowd. 'We'll look after you, Violet,' he assured me, and I believe they would have done; they were nice chaps. But I felt that God gave me the strength to refuse, even though I was sometimes lonely, because I knew it would be wrong for me as a Christian to be seen getting mixed up in some of the things that went on. But sometimes I felt I was fighting a lone battle on all fronts.

I knew army life wouldn't go on for ever, and in 1947 my demob papers came through so that meant I'd be back in Civvie Street.

I had a job lined up to go to. I had kept in touch with the ladies who ran the Christian club in London, where I sometimes used to play the piano when I was at Moray Lodge. One of them who had been a missionary before the war had a friend who had also been a missionary but was living now with her husband and small son near Tunbridge Wells in Kent. This couple wanted to bring the Christian message to the village children in their area. My job would be to help them in this work and to do some domestic work for them, and this seemed an ideal way forward for me. It was a bit like being a missionary in my own country.

Meanwhile things at Chequers weren't any easier on the domestic front. One morning, not long before I was due to leave, two of Mr Attlee's private detectives came to see me. They asked if I would be prepared to stay if the Prime Minister himself asked me. I told them I had a job to go to, but if they liked to wait I'd phone and check whether it was definite. So I rang the lady in question and asked, 'Are you expecting me?'

She immediately said, 'Yes.'

So when I rang off I turned to the detectives and said, 'Gentlemen, there is your answer.'

I have to admit that if they had laid their cards on the table earlier on I might have stayed. But the workload was too great. I could have managed my own job, but doing all the extra because these new girls weren't prepared to do it, exhausted me. I thought no one realised what the situation was, and I felt relieved when the demob officer said to me, 'We knew what was going on, Pond, but there was nothing we could do about it.'

ERNEST BEVIN

Ernest Bevin crossed Violet's path when she was at Chequers. He was Minister of Labour and National Service in Churchill's wartime cabinet and would often visit on weekends. After the war he was Foreign Secretary in Clement Attlee's Labour cabinet and asked Violet to work for him in his London home.

I wasn't short of choices for the future – I was offered a job in the London home of Mr Ernest Bevin, who was Foreign Secretary in Mr Attlee's government at the time. I had a look at the house and I knew it wasn't right for me.

But all my life I had wanted to do missionary work and now I had the opportunity. I felt reassured that I'd made the right decision when I remembered a verse I know that tells us how God leads his children step by step. I knew that was true even though I didn't know then what future steps might be. I've often thought of what our teachers told us at Sunday School when we were children – 'Always aim high' – and I suppose you could say that I've tried to make that my motto in life.

10

ARMY DAYS ARE OVER

My life in the army was over. So off I went to Slough to be demobbed.

We were allowed to keep our greatcoat but no other uniform. Clothes were still rationed, but we were supplied with clothing coupons and an allowance to buy the essentials. So I needed to go shopping as soon as possible, and with that in mind I went to stay with Auntie who lived near Brixton in South London.

CLOTHES AND FASHION IN THE FORTIES

Clothing coupons were issued in 1941 when clothes rationing began, and the allowance was gradually cut until in 1945 each person had to manage on only thirty-six coupons a year. A woman's tweed suit cost eighteen coupons, a woollen dress eleven, a skirt seven and a blouse or a cardigan five. Buying a pair of shoes used up seven. So make-do-and-mend was the order of the day with stockings being endlessly repaired, and a father's worn shirt remade into a blouse for his daughter. Wartime brides often borrowed a wedding dress to save

143

their coupons for a going-away outfit. The government introduced a 'Utility' range of clothes and furniture, with a controlled price tag. Utility clothes made by quality fashion firms represented really good value because these houses were not prepared to lower their standards even when they produced clothes for the utility market.

Australians were allowed to send wool or material to their poorly dressed friends in Britain, but Lady Astor was fined £50 (ten times the cost of a lady's suit) after she had persuaded American friends to send her ready-made clothes from the United States. There were clothing regulations in America too, controlling the quantity of cloth that could be used in a garment and forbidding the use of 'fabric on fabric', or any added trimmings.

There was a department store in the High Street and a row of other shops, so Auntie and I went into one of them and asked to see some coats. The assistant brought some for me to see, but all I could say was, 'These aren't any good to me.' I knew I would feel the cold after being in army uniform, and also I couldn't abide anything that was not quality.

'Did you want a heavier coat?' the assistant asked, and when I agreed, she disappeared into the back regions. She came back bringing a wonderful Harris tweed coat in blue.

'Now that's more like it!' I exclaimed as I tried it on.

Well, I bought it, and it took every penny of my demob money – and I didn't bat an eyelid. I think the truth of the matter is that I'd got used to seeing good clothes and couldn't bear to have something that was poor quality. So I began to save up to buy a hat to match (we all wore hats whenever we went out in those days). Then I saved up again and paid the earth for a blue handbag and finally, in Tunbridge Wells, I saw a marvellous blue suit and bought that too. That suit lasted me years because being still in service I only wore it on my half-day off. For quite a while I used to wait till I had enough money to choose really good, quality garments, but in the end I came down to earth and went back to ordinary, less expensive clothes once again.

Fashion picture from 1940s

I was with the missionary friends near Tunbridge Wells for about three years, but I have to admit that by 1950 I was getting a bit unsettled and I took it into my head to get in touch again with Mrs Hill, the curator at Chequers, and ask if she knew of any jobs that would suit me. She suggested the Church of England Clergy Home at Ellesborough Manor. It's just across the road from the church which the Prime Minister attends when he's at Chequers and near all my old haunts. So I took the bull by the horns, applied for the job and got it. Soon I was back in my favourite county of Buckinghamshire ('Bucks is best' is one of my mottoes).

ELLESBOROUGH

Violet shared the Attlees' love of the country around Chequers, in the county of Buckinghamshire, returning in 1950 for fourteen years. A hundred years before Violet's time George Lipscombe described the area, in a prosaic account that nonetheless rings with the poetry of its place-names: 'Ellesborough is situated ... at the foot of the Chiltern Hills, about four miles SSE of Aylesbury, and two miles west of Wendover. This parish, with its hamlets, is bounded, on the north by Stoke-Mandeville; on the east by Wendover; on the south by the Hampdens; and on the west by the Kimbles.'

The church of St Peter and St Paul at Ellesborough, where, until Tony Blair's premiership, Prime Ministers have attended Sunday service, has its own ghost – a man dressed in medieval clothes who glides into the church, stopping only at a memorial plaque before disappearing into thin air. Not many have seen the ghost, but an organist preparing for Sunday worship, a lady arranging the flowers for the church, and in 1970 someone in the graveyard, have all been unexpectedly surprised by the silent visitor to the quiet church.

Ellesborough Manor at that time was a retirement home for clergy, and my main work was to serve two meals a day as well as see to the cleaning. The dining-room had twelve little tables, each seating two people. I enjoyed serving meals in style to clergy who had worked hard all their lives and who really appreciated it. But the rooms weren't easy to clean, and the girls who helped me were not trained in the old ways. They would throw around the china and glass and put things back on the shelves still dripping. I was within cycling distance once more of Risborough Baptist Church, where I used to belong when I was at Chequers.

I was there for about eight years, and there was only one snag – serving dinner at night meant that I wasn't free in the evenings. So I couldn't join in fully with the life of the church as I would have liked to do.

Eventually, someone heard me say that I would like a job along the Risborough Road, nearer the church, and told me that there was a job going just in the area I had in mind. No sooner said than done. I applied and was called for an interview with Mrs Money-Coutts. She came from the Hobhouse family in Somerset and was an 'honourable' in her own right, as was Mr Money-Coutts. Their son, David, who was a young man then, was working in Coutts bank. (He went on to become banker to the Queen until he retired in 2003. It was many years later that I saw him again, when I attended the funeral of Mr Money-Coutts. I couldn't believe my eyes – he was the image of his father in the days when I had been with the family.)

At my interview Mr Money-Coutts asked me if I liked children. Their daughters were about nine and ten. I wasn't sure what he meant by the question so I just told him that I had two nieces of my own and that seemed to satisfy them – that and the fact that when I'd met the girls I'd treated them naturally with no extra fuss. I discovered afterwards that the person they'd had before me had rather spoilt the girls and bought them presents and things, and the parents didn't approve of that. Although they never went short of anything, Mr and Mrs Money-Coutts treated the girls very wisely.

The whole family was very fond of animals, but not sloppy about them, and they had horses and ponies. If one of the girls asked for something, pleading that some other child had got it, their mother would say, 'Now look, you have a pony, you have a dog and you can't have other things you want as well. It's either-or, but not both.'

I laid my cards on the table at the interview and told them that I would want to be free to go to church in the evenings, and that suited Mrs Money-Coutts because she liked to cook the evening meal herself. She said that she didn't want the children getting used to the idea that there was always domestic help at hand, in case the time came when they couldn't afford it.

I got the job, and after I'd started work Mrs Money-Coutts told me that at the interview I almost convinced her that she needed me more than I needed her! I can't think what she meant! But my terms suited her anyway, so she engaged me. I was the only servant living in, but Mrs Bounds came in daily. She lived in a cottage at the top of the drive, which belonged to the house. She used to do the bedrooms, and I did the downstairs rooms.

Once more I was spared doing the cooking because Mrs Money-Coutts liked to do it herself. She always seemed to leave the preparing till the last minute. I'd have one eye on the clock and wonder however she was going to get the meal on time. Then she would suddenly burst through the door, dash out into the garden and come back laden with vegetables, and in no time they'd be in the pot and merrily boiling away.

Occasionally I would sit with the children if Mrs Money-Coutts was going out, but she always managed to discover which evenings I had something on at the church and never ever asked me to 'sit' on those nights; she made other arrangements. She never stood in my way.

She helped me a lot in other ways too. I wanted to make the best I could of myself, and she would help by gently putting me right if I used a word wrongly or by correcting my grammar. They really took an interest in what I was trying to do, which was to gain more Bible knowledge and learn how to communicate.

When I heard that our minister was holding a Baptist Union class, I joined it. Soon after that I saw a course of evening classes advertised by the London Bible College, and I signed up for that. I spent all my savings on fares to London and the cost of the course – but it was worth every penny!

At the end of the year came the exam. We all sat waiting nervously for it to begin, and I started thinking how silly I was to imagine I could pass. Just at that moment one of the lecturers came into the room. I don't know why, but he looked right across at me and gave me a lovely smile. And I thought, 'Get on with it, Violet, you can do it!' And I did. I passed and I have the certificate to prove it.

After that, though, I did get a bit bogged down, not finding a suitable course to follow on with, and one or two schemes fell flat. I didn't lose my faith, but I did begin to wonder in what direction God wanted me to go.

One day at church, when I was feeling really down about things, a friend marched me down the path and pushed me in at the front door of the Manse as if to say to the Minister, 'You cope with her!' And he did. He finally got out of me what was troubling me and said, 'We'll think and pray about it. Meanwhile there's a need for more lay preachers in Buckingham, and I'm going to put your name down on my list.'

I hadn't thought about doing this kind of work, but the minister's plans went ahead. I thought, 'If I'm going in for that sort of thing, I need to be able to speak well; people will want to be able to hear me clearly.' So a lady I knew gave me lessons in that.

Later on I was actually elected as president of the lay preachers for a year's term of office. The Money-Coutts were really thrilled for me. I bought a new hat for the occasion, and Mrs Money-Coutts insisted on ushering me out of the *front* door.

Mrs Money-Coutts helped me in so many ways. She knew I wanted to get experience in an office job, so she told me I could have some hours off every week and not lose any of my wages. I heard of a little job going in Aylesbury and got it, so off I used to go once a week and try my hand at dealing with invoices, for gaskets and those sort of things.

I had been with the family for six years and was very happy, but I got to a point where I was feeling a bit battered and exhausted. Clifford and I have always kept closely in touch, and, as usual in my times of need, he took over. He told me to pack up my things and go to stay with him and his family and have everything done for me until I was rested and a bit stronger. It worked out well because it turned out that Mrs Money-Coutts didn't really need me any longer but hadn't liked to tell me. The girls were older, and she was determined that they should learn to fend for themselves to prepare them for the future if need be. So once again I left Buckinghamshire and stayed with Clifford and Muriel while I got my strength back. I wondered just what direction my life would take next.

The answer was Woolworth's! I got a job there once I was feeling stronger, and it gave me good experience in dealing with the public, coping with money and figures and also in ordering and in setting out books – my favourite part of the job.

Then at last I had the opportunity to get my first office job, and I felt I was getting nearer to my goal because it was with a missionary society, Wycliffe Bible Translators.

WYCLIFFE BIBLE TRANSLATORS

'If your God is so great, why can't he speak my language?' That was the question Cameron Townsend was asked by a member of the Cakchiquel Indians when he arrived in 1917 as a missionary in Guatemala, selling Bibles in Spanish.

It took Cameron ten years to learn their language and translate the New Testament for them. Once a church had been firmly established, he left to continue the work of translating the Bible into other languages, some difficult to learn, others never before written down. So Cameron and his colleagues devised a course to provide the necessary training. Wycliffe Bible Translators was formed in the United States and the Summer Institute of Linguistics (SIL) set up in 1934. Wycliffe UK was formed in 1964, and is part of Wycliffe International.

Mr Campbell Reid was my boss, and when I started he said to me, 'You may wonder how you got this job as there were about eight applicants – well, all the others dropped out, except you.' That's one way of succeeding!

I ended up in accounts, and Mr Reid was a wonderful teacher. He really gave me confidence. In those days it was a matter of adding up long columns of figures on great big sheets of paper. Just imagine having no calculators or computers to do the work for you! Do you know, Mr Reid was so good at it that he would just stand by the door and look across at my sheet of figures and tell from there if I'd got it right. He taught me the art of adding up those long columns, and although he was so good at it himself and I was a beginner, he never ever made me feel silly.

Mr Reid used to give two of us a lift to work every day. He and Mrs Reid had a boarding-house, and we boarded there, but when they moved house it meant I would have a very awkward journey on the buses to get to work.

So I got another job in Surrey, with my old friends of the National Young Life Campaign, and once again I was working in the accounts department. It must seem as though my life has been made up of lots of bits and pieces with all the changes I've had, but I can see how all the different experiences have added up and prepared me for what was to come next.

NATIONAL YOUNG LIFE CAMPAIGN

In the early years of the last century, two brothers – Frederick and Arthur Wood – set out to work for evangelism among the young people of Britain. One day, as they travelled together by train, they discussed their vision for youth work, and Arthur traced the initials YLC on the misted carriage window. This was to become the symbol of the movement when it came into being in 1911, supported by an imposing group of evangelical bishops and churchmen.

The work gathered momentum, and the brothers held rallies in cities and towns in Britain, the United States and Canada. During World War II, YLC leaders decided to direct their efforts to work among the Armed Forces in Britain. Centres, known as Forces Institutes, were set up near main camps, and by 1944 there were fourteen of such centres with a thousand men and women attending one of them every night. In one small centre 50,000 troops passed through in the space of eleven months.

Today NYLC is known as Young Life and is still working at seaside missions, camps and wherever young people are to be found.

Their office was in Kingston, so the next problem was finding somewhere to live because housing was still in short supply, but in the end I managed to get digs.

All was well for a couple of years until I found out that the owner of the house where I was in lodgings was moving away and I'd have to find other accommodation. Some friends of mine had just got married (they were full of the joys of spring), and they'd managed to get a house through some friends at the church, but there wasn't much hope for single people. The YWCA was only intended to house young women, not those in their forties like me and some of my friends, who were in the same boat. I even got in touch with our local MP and told him about the situation, but although he was sympathetic he couldn't help.

While I was wondering whatever to do next, someone showed me an advertisement in a Christian newspaper about some new flats near Ipswich. They were for missionaries and Christian workers who had retired and were prepared to help with Christian work in the surrounding villages. I thought, why not have a go and apply? I had nothing to lose but the price of a stamp. Clifford was dubious because I was not retired, and, in fact, he phoned the manager, Mr Goddard, to make sure they knew that. But Mr Goddard's reply was, 'Tell her to come and see us.'

So I went to Ipswich, and Mr Goddard explained that although the new flats were for retired people only, the manager was free to house anyone, without restrictions, in the original old house. He told me on the spot that there was a flat there for me if I wanted it and if I would be willing to help with some Christian work among children in the villages around. Of course, that was just up my street, and I didn't take long to make up my mind.

My newly married friends didn't agree with the move, and in fact they called on me at midnight the very night before I left, to let me know that God had told them I ought not to go. I'm not sure why they were so keen for me not to go. It may have been that they thought Datchet was too ecumenical. I thanked them very much for their trouble but did not change my mind. I was so sure that I was doing the right thing that I was not too upset by their visit.

When I told Auntie, in London, that I was moving to Ipswich, she said, 'Why Ipswich, dear?' I told her that I felt sure that it was the right place for me to go so she just said, 'Oh well, you'll meet somebody there, no doubt.' But at this stage I certainly never thought I'd ever get married.

❧ *11* ❧

ROMANCE

*N*o sooner had I arrived at the Datchet Evangelical Fellowship and settled into my flat than I was met by more doubts and fears from other people. The general verdict was, 'You won't get a job – not here in Ipswich.'

DATCHET HOUSE – RURAL MINISTRIES

Datchet Evangelical Fellowship was founded by Mr Goddard with the aim of strengthening village churches through the help of Christian leaders and workers who were retired but still active. New flats were built, and Datchet House itself divided up to provide extra accommodation for willing volunteers. The work of the fellowship has continued and is thriving, now with the new name of Rural Ministries. The headquarters are still in Ipswich, but the work has spread beyond East Anglia and personnel are now working in different parts of England. The aim is still to support and strengthen existing rural churches as well as to maintain a Christian witness in Britain's villages. Local fellowships are set up which in time become independent churches.

Nothing daunted, I trawled Ipswich for several days and did manage to get a job, in a book shop. Books have followed me all my life and I have always loved them. I was to work in accounts again, something I was used to by this time. The shop was in a beautiful old building, called Ancient House, and Charles II had hidden there. (Up in the attic there was an effigy of him, hiding.) So, to most people's amazement, I'd got a flat and a job too.

The bookshop was owned by a Col. Langley. I knew that he had been in the Army and was evacuated at Dunkirk, but it was only recently that I heard more about him. There was a television programme shown in 2004 in which Lieutenant Jimmy Langley, as he was then, was featured as one of the officers who had played a very brave part in that operation. I didn't know at the time I worked there that his wife had been in the French Resistance. They had a son of about sixteen who used to come into the shop; he often used to ask me about the war during our coffee break. He'd say, 'Sit back and tell me what it was really like.'

Col. Langley was very gentlemanly, but I remember he once let out a swear word when we were cashing up as usual at the end of the week. He apologised by saying, 'Sorry, Miss Pond, but I was in the Army.' To reassure him I said, 'And I was in the ATS.'

After I'd been at Datchet some little while, a strange incident took place. After listening to a sermon in church – a sermon I've long since forgotten – I knew in my heart of hearts that I had to be willing to say to God that I would give up my flat if that was what he wanted. It seemed a strange message. Could it mean that at last God would call me to missionary work? That was one explanation. But whatever the reason might turn out to be, I just knew I had to be willing to give up the flat. And I *did* love my flat! By the time I got out of church, I couldn't speak until I'd said, 'Yes, Lord, you can have it.'

LIVING AT DATCHET

Beryl Lawson, then Beryl Goddard, the daughter of the founder, remembers Violet well, even though her stay at Datchet was only a short one. She still speaks warmly of the 'gentle, friendly, kindly lady whose faith in Christ showed not only in her features but also in her actions'. She has never forgotten Violet's timely help: 'Violet noticed how busy I was in helping both with the administration of Rural Ministries (then known as Datchet Evangelical Fellowship) and in caring for my parents and she asked me if I would like her to clean my flat each week for no charge. I was overwhelmed by her perception and kindness and gladly accepted. But Violet's kindness to me personally was typical of her.'

One morning not long afterwards, I was walking up the lane as usual to catch the bus to work. It had been snowing, and I noticed footprints in the snow. I could tell that someone from our block of flats had been this way before me. When I climbed onto the bus I saw who it was. His name was Fred Liddle, and he'd moved into one of the flats in the new block because his wife was very ill in the local hospital. He was terribly distressed because she didn't even recognise him any longer. Not wanting to get involved, I went right to the front of the bus, as far away from him as possible. Then later on I heard that she'd died, and that he was staying on in the flat.

One Sunday morning a good while later on, having decided not to go to church for some reason, I was sitting in the residents' lounge when Fred Liddle walked in.

'Not at church this morning?' he asked.

We talked for a bit. I discovered his wife had not known him for quite a long time before her death, and he felt as if he had lost her years before.

After we'd chatted for a while the time was getting on, and he asked, 'Well, what are you having for dinner?'

'I've got a tin and a tin-opener and a packet of crisps at the ready,' I replied.

'That's no good to anyone,' he said, 'why don't you come and have dinner with me?'

I saw no reason why not. We were all familiar faces, living in the same Datchet complex, so it seemed quite proper to accept the invitation, and I went across to his flat for Sunday dinner.

I noticed a cloth on the windowsill and realised it was a bit out of some old pyjamas. Fred had been busy cleaning. (We used to make do with all sorts of worn-out clothing to use as cleaning rags.) Mind you, those old pyjamas were quickly whisked out of sight when he realised he'd left them there by mistake. So he seemed to be good around the house. I noticed in the kitchen that he was a proper bachelor cook. He had one saucepan with three compartments, so that he could cook all the vegetables at one time.

We got on really well. You could say that we just seemed to 'click'. Even so you could have knocked me down with a feather when, out of the blue, before that afternoon was over, he said, 'You and I are going to get married.'

No one could imagine what a shock it was to me. So I suppose it's every bit as surprising that I agreed to his proposal.

The strange thing was that in spite of it being so sudden, I never for one moment doubted that he'd got it right. And from that day on our friendship steadily grew and we never looked back. Although it must have seemed sudden to other people too, I don't remember that anyone ever told us we ought to take our time or stop and think longer about it. It just seemed as right to them as it did to us.

We used to meet on a Thursday, which was the day that Fred came into Ipswich to do his shopping. I'd see him from the shop, swinging his brief case (because he wouldn't be seen with a shopping bag), and we'd go to the Chinese restaurant for lunch.

I wrote to tell Clifford, though the news finally reached him in a rather roundabout way. Somehow my letter had got misdirected, so when he finally got it, the postman handed it to my brother in person. The date was April the first – April Fools' Day! When Clifford opened it and saw my request for him to give me away at my wedding, he was so overcome and excited that he ran after the postman to tell him what good news he'd brought. Fred's minister was delighted too when Fred told him that he was marrying Pastor Pond's sister, because Clifford is well-known in our church circles.

Of course I was longing for him to meet Fred, so it was arranged that Clifford and Muriel would come across to Ipswich. I asked my boss for the day off work and explained that I had to see my brother urgently. I never let on why, but I found out that everyone in the office knew all about it anyway. They had seen Fred and me meeting on a Thursday and guessed that romance was in the air.

The four of us went to the Chinese restaurant, and I need have had no worries. We got on together famously, and in fact we had a hilarious time over lunch.

Violet and Fred's wedding

Then Auntie met Fred and she approved of him too. That was important to me because both my parents had died by this time and what Auntie thought mattered a lot. She was Mother's sister at Brixham, who'd always been so good to me.

It was on one of the days when Fred and I were going for lunch that I suddenly spotted a dress in the window of Richard's. 'There's my dress!' I thought. I knew at once it was the right one for my wedding. So I went in and put down a deposit and paid the rest when I collected it later. My two nieces were highly amused and couldn't believe it when they found that their aunt's dress was shorter than theirs. But at least I managed to get them out of jeans and into dresses for the day, to be my bridesmaids.

Fred and I had a simple wedding, but it was just right – I wouldn't have changed a thing. We were so happy! We had a great, great marriage and just over ten wonderful years together.

We travelled and went to Germany for three weeks to visit Fred's son in the army there. I was able to use all the different skills and experience I'd gained up to now to help Fred. Although he'd had a slight stroke already he had fully recovered, and it was only towards the end that he was ill, and then it meant that I was able to nurse him. So what have I got to complain about? Nothing!

At first we were allocated a double flat at Datchet, in the same complex, and I settled down to married life. Only one thing spoiled our comfort, and that was that the flat suffered terribly from the effects of condensation. The walls ran with water and everything felt damp. It was only a small thing in the order of things, but it did make life difficult. (Well, we need some pinpricks, don't we, when everything is so good otherwise. It stops us forgetting God and our need of him.)

Eventually, when the rules for residents were changed, I felt I couldn't go on living there. So Fred spoke to the person who had been his boss when he worked for the Shaftesbury Society. They had begun their housing scheme of homes for older people, and because he'd worked for them, Fred's name was put down for a flat in the first block they built, in Croydon, Surrey. And that was where we went.

I was asked to be warden of the flats until someone permanent was found. That meant keeping an eye on the older residents and being on hand for any emergency when help might be needed. Once a regular warden was appointed, I acted as voluntary stand-in for when the warden was off duty or away. Fred was pleased about that and it suited me well.

Fred still did quite a bit of preaching, and I often went with him. I remember once when he'd been asked to speak about his mission work in London, and he went on a bit about the rats – and how you could see their eyes shining in the dark. I thought perhaps it was a bit much for some of the old ladies and when he asked one of them afterwards if she'd enjoyed the meeting she said: 'No I didn't! Talking about *rats*!'

'Well,' he said, 'if I'd been giving a talk on Africa it would have been lions, but in London it's rats!'

I thought it best to get him away quickly after that. So although I didn't become a missionary myself, I married one.

And Fred's work had been real missionary work, even though it wasn't in foreign lands.

It was while we were living in Croydon that Fred died. It happened like this. His health had been failing, and I had been so glad of the nursing skills I'd picked up along the way so that I could look after him. An elderly lady living in the flats, who was in her nineties, used to love to call on us in the evenings. She'd spend a bit of time with us, talking and being sociable. One evening she was there while Fred was sitting in his chair as usual. I had slipped out of the room for a moment when I heard the old lady saying in an agitated way, 'Mr Liddle, speak to me! Speak to me!' I rushed back to the room and could see immediately that it was serious. I phoned for an ambulance. They came quickly, but Fred was dead before they even got him to the hospital.

I remember getting back from the hospital finally to find a few of our friends along with the warden who had been waiting for me in the residents' lounge. We prayed together and it was so good to have their support. I suppose the shock didn't set in until later. I had decided to give a little gift to the ambulance people who had been so kind, but when a friend took me to the ambulance station I suddenly found that I could hardly climb the steps, it seemed as if my legs would give way under me. The lady there said, 'Arthritis, dear?' and I saw the funny side of that even then.

I was allowed to stay on in the double flat, but there were two snags. One was the fact that I was using space that a couple might need, and also the rent was more than I could afford. Then I was told that the Croydon Home was to be closed down anyway, and we were to be transferred to other Shaftesbury homes. I was taken by car to see the brand new homes at Wandsworth in South London. The road they were in was terrible and so was the view from the building. I took one look at it through the car window and refused to get out to look any further. Anyway, I really wanted to move nearer my old haunts north of London.

There was a big meeting about it all, and Muriel, Clifford's wife, came too. She calmed me down and suggested we look at the full list of Shaftesbury homes. She pointed out one near Aylesbury. 'You always liked Aylesbury,' she said, 'see if you can get a flat there.' And the good news was that a single flat was found for me, in my favourite county of Buckinghamshire, so back I went, on home ground once again.

This chapter would not really be complete without something more about Fred himself. In about 1970, he wrote down an account of his life, much of it spent as a missionary in London. I'm including excerpts from these memoirs to give you a better glimpse of the wonderful man I loved and married.

FRED'S OWN STORY

I was born in 1904 on a cold December day above a stable, where you could hear the neighing and kicking of the horses below. My father drove a gig and four-in-hand for his master, a local doctor, in the dark and dismal pit village of South Moor near Stanley in County Durham.

What stands out in my memory as a young child was the fact that my mother was a Christian but my father was often drunk and spent much of his money on horse racing. My mother would take me – holding my hand in hers – to the Wesleyan chapel at Stanley, where we sat Sunday by Sunday in the gallery. I believe that my mother's prayers were answered when, on 24 June 1920, at the age of sixteen, I accepted Jesus Christ as my Lord and Saviour.

Early next morning at half-past four, I went to the pit as usual but I felt a new person – as if I was walking on air. All my work mates, who knew me well, laughed when I tried to explain to them how the chains of sin had been broken and that from now on I wanted to live for Christ. But as time went on they were able to see for themselves what a great change God had brought about in my life.

When I was eighteen I was called and trained to be a local preacher in the Methodist Church, and six years later God called me to mission work in London. I was accepted by the London City Mission in November 1929.

The Mission stood near the site of the baker's shop where the Great Fire of London started in 1666 and was the old district of Charles Dickens' *Oliver Twist,* with its slums and tenements, where ragged urchins, dirty and dishevelled, lay at night under the railway arches of the City and Metropolitan lines.

I was within five minutes' walk of St Paul's Cathedral, at the heart of the great city of London. I felt a great sense of privilege at being called to work here, and as I walked around the district I felt the presence of Christ and his nearness in all my work. Alcohol, drugs and meths-drinking were rampant among the people who lived in these back alleys and streets.

One of the first people I met in this district was a cat-burglar who became a Christian. He and his wife joined the Mission and later became its caretakers.

Another strange character was Mr Dacks. He had been a scrap-metal merchant in his young days and was often the worse for drink, which had reduced him to poverty and shame.

I was asked to visit him in a top back room. I knocked at the door and a rough, harsh voice said, 'Come in!' I opened the door and saw a man of about fifty sitting on a box which served for a chair; in one corner were two sacks of old iron and in another a single bed, with bedding that had not been washed for weeks. In another corner, fastened to a chain, was a wild-looking tabby cat, which arched its back and spat at me. It could not have been out for weeks on end because the smell was horrific.

After further visits I was able, with God's help, to win Mr Dacks' confidence and become his friend. I arranged to have his room cleaned out and papered and obtained some clothes for him. He began coming to the Mission and one Sunday he gave his life to the Lord Jesus and was a changed man.

Another personality I met in 1930 was Mrs Lucy. She had been an invalid for fourteen years and lived in one room with a dog, two bantam hens and a canary in a cage, with hardly a feather on it. When her husband had been alive he had mended old shoes, then sold them cheaply to poor people. After he died she tried to carry on the business alone but one day she had a fall. She was a heavy woman, and she stepped on a floor board which gave way because of dry rot; her leg went down the hole and she sprained her hip. She managed to haul herself up and crawl to her bed in the little room behind the shop, where she lay for sixteen years until her death. Every Monday for nearly three years I used to call on her, and she too found Jesus as her Saviour. I used to sing her favourite hymns to her from Sankey's hymn-book and read to her from the Bible.

The street she lived in was noted at that time for having the worst rate of tuberculosis. There were costers, market men and women, and railway men, all with great social and spiritual needs. This was God in the slums, at work among all kinds of people in the common round of everyday life.

From 1934 until 1940 we worked in the great Meat Market of Smithfield. There at the hub of the metropolis, men and women, boys and girls came onto the Mission premises and heard the gospel, and many responded to it.

Then came the Second World War. The railway tunnels nearby were used as air raid shelters, and seven hundred people would come to shelter from the bombing. Every evening I was able to go around, supplying cups of tea and food as well as telling people the Good News about my Saviour and Lord. We also lent blankets to those who hadn't any, thanks to the kindness of the Mennonite Church in Canada who supplied them.

Twice, during the bombing of London, I was blown off my feet by the blast, but I suffered nothing but shock, and I believe that God was preserving me for the work he still had for me to do.

Then, on 10 May 1940, I stood in the market place at nine o'clock in the morning and looked helplessly at the burning ruins of our dear Mission. It had been set on fire by bombs during the night. There were tears in my eyes as I stood there. But God was good, and we were able to carry on the work, later joining the Great Arthur Street Mission in Moreland Street, East London.

I soon discovered that I had arrived in answer to the prayers of two saintly ladies who had been endeavouring to keep the Mission open and running, doing what they could until they were evacuated to Sussex. When I went to see them they told me that they had been praying night and day for someone to come and take their place and carry on the work of the Mission. It was situated not far from the old hall in City Road where

William Booth of the Salvation Army had begun his work in the nineteenth century. It was here that Salvationists were pelted with eggs and tomatoes when they witnessed for Christ.

A very old Baptist Church provided us with premises, though it was now battered by the blitz; but I was able to lay the foundation with the few people left from the two missions. After two or three years it became known as the Finsbury Mission, a branch of the Shaftesbury Mission. I fixed a loudspeaker in the old tower on the Mission building and broadcast recorded hymns and a message every lunch-hour between twelve noon and one o'clock. This was the time that workers in the nearby gin factory sat outside to eat their sandwiches and could listen in.

One day I was called upon to take sixteen boys to Pinewood Film Studios; they had been chosen to act as Fagin's boys in a scene from the Rank Organization film *Oliver*. They had to go just as they were dressed at home, and they all looked and acted their part well.

On a Sunday evening, after the service at the Mission, I used to hold a Bible quiz in the local pub nearby. We used to go with the thirty or forty who had been at our service, and when we arrived at the public house there would be fifty or sixty in the bar parlour. There were tears on the cheeks of quite a few when members of our choir sang 'The Old Rugged Cross'. I am sure that Jesus would have done the same if he had been in our place, and we felt God was very present. Gradually the Mission became known as a spiritual centre in the borough of Finsbury, and on more than one occasion the mayor and his dignitaries were present at our services. We tried to care for the young people, children and older folk day by day in every way that met their needs.

We carried on our work even in the days of the pilotless planes, known as 'doodlebugs'. There were many opportunities to minister to those around us who were bombed out and sent on to our local centre. We would help them to search among the debris for their broken treasured objects, bring them comfort from God's Word as well as giving them all the practical help we could.

Then early one morning at about six o'clock, one of these planes dropped next door to my own home near the Mission and blasted us out of bed. My wife and I escaped with only a few scratches, but two of the people opposite us were killed outright. These were the days when we saw the Cockney spirit shown by all around us and their courage under such great strain. Our Mission doors were open during all the days of the blitz, to help all we could and meet the needs as far as possible. It was wonderful, amidst all the dust and grime of bombed buildings, to feel God's presence very close to us.

In May 1948, I was sent to my present Mission in Notting Hill where I have been able to serve for twenty years. This district is completely different from my last one, and the people were very reluctant to talk. When I first arrived I felt that I would never break through. Then one day I called together a number of men and women, about twenty in all, grandparents of the children around us. With the help of the borough we started a lunch centre – the first of its kind in the district – which grew from twenty members to over one hundred and seventy. This opened the door for me to reach the parents through the older folk, and many found help and cheer as well as God's blessing through the club.

This area was known for its gypsies who lived in caravans under the railway arches. It was their sons and daughters who became scrap merchants. One lady – a real Romany – lived in a caravan behind the Mission and attended the services, accepting Jesus Christ as her Saviour. She was suddenly taken ill one day and rushed to hospital where she remained unconscious for over a week. I visited her two or three times, once when her eldest son was there too. Days later I went again, and she had still not opened her eyes. I went behind the curtains round her bed and prayed over her. When I had finished she opened her eyes and said 'Mr Liddle!' then asked for a drink. When I told the ward sister, she could not believe me until she saw for herself. That evening her son came to the Mission to thank me because his mother had 'returned from the dead' through my prayers, but I told him it was not my doing but God's. She lived another three years but one cold winter she was found in her caravan asleep, it seemed, with a lovely smile on her face. Her heavenly Father had taken her home. At her funeral tears fell down the cheeks of the costers gathered there to pay their last respects to a great old lady as we sang her favourite hymn – 'What a Friend We Have in Jesus'.

Later the neighbourhood changed as many immigrants moved into the district. Here I had an opportunity to meet the needs of some of them in my daily work, and children and adults joined the Mission activities. Racial riots that flared up died down as people learned to live and intermingle with the newcomers.

After we had been there eighteen years the Mission building was demolished and moved into new premises nearby. A new motorway was to be built and the area redeveloped. This was a great upheaval for those who had lived many years in the same district. But change has to come and the work of the Mission continued and our God remains unchanging.

—From Fred Liddle's unpublished memoirs

SHADES OF THE PAST

*A*fter Fred had died and I had moved to Aylesbury, Clifford and Muriel came to visit me one day and asked if I'd like to have a run around my old haunts in their car. I was very keen to renew old memories, and I had a special hankering to see Ayot St Lawrence once again. I suppose it must have been forty years since I'd worked there, but it had played a big part in my life, and I wondered if it would still have the same appeal for me. By this time the house was in the hands of the National Trust, as Mr Shaw had wished it to be. It had been kept as much as possible like it was when the Shaws were there. A custodian lives on the premises, and it is opened to the public.

THE NATIONAL TRUST

'Mark my words, Miss Hill, this is going to be a very big thing.' The Duke of Westminster was speaking to Octavia Hill as plans to found the National Trust began to unfold. Octavia had long worked for the homeless in London, and as well as providing dwellings in Paradise

Place and making them habitable, she had created a garden out of an old dumping-ground, for parents and children alike to enjoy.

The foundation of the Trust took place in the Duke of Westminster's London home, Grosvenor Place, in 1895. Since then, it has protected and preserved for the nation many beautiful gardens and homes as well as almost six hundred miles of coast and thousands of acres of countryside. All the properties are excellently maintained, and many have splendid restaurants and tea-rooms as well as shops, to complete the enjoyment of a day out. The National Trust has no government help and relies entirely on its more than three million members and supporters for its costly maintenance.

It was typical that we arrived on a day when the house was closed to visitors, but I knew too that I wasn't likely to get another chance to visit, so I decided to knock on the door and see what happened.

When the custodian opened it, I peered inside. I realised straight away that the piano was not where it used to be.

'The piano shouldn't be there,' I told him.

He looked a bit surprised and said 'You'd better come in,' and we did.

When he discovered who we were, he explained that the piano had been moved from its original place so as to give a clear passage to visitors coming through. That I could understand.

Then he began to ask about other things and was only too keen to make good use of all my memories, so that they could keep everything as much as possible the way it had been in the old days.

They asked me to come back and tell them more, but I said I had no means of getting there from my flat in Aylesbury.

'No problem,' they assured me, 'we'll fetch you and take you back.'

And that is what they did.

Every year they held a coffee morning for all the voluntary workers, just before the house reopened after the winter break. They used to invite me to come and answer questions, especially from the new workers who were going to show the public around, and wanted to get all the details right.

More recently, Stephen Bennett, who was the current National Trust custodian, asked me over. After he'd shown me around, he tape-recorded some of my memories of life with Mr and Mrs Shaw. I was delighted with the way that the garden has now been restored to just the way it was in Mr Shaw's time.

Shaw's Corner in 2003

Then he asked if I'd attend on the opening day of a special event in August, called 'Living with the Shaws'. I went over with some of my friends, and I sat in the kitchen and chatted to all the visitors, answering questions and doing my bit. It was exhausting but exciting too.

SHAW'S CORNER

'Has such a trifle any use or interest for the National Trust?' Shaw wrote, only a few weeks after Charlotte had died. He was suggesting that the Trust should take over Shaw's Corner after his death. The National Trust accepted his offer, and Shaw set about collecting busts and pictures and statuettes from the London flat to 'titivate Shaw's Corner as a showplace'.

Today Shaw's Corner is a delightful place to visit, approached down narrow lanes, where Shaw once cycled and T. E. Lawrence roared along on his motorcycle, Boanerges. Inside the entrance hall Shaw's hats still hang on the hat-stand. Violet remembers that he wore wool hats in summer and straw hats in winter. Everything has been left as far as possible as it was in the Shaws' day, except that Charlotte's room has been made into a museum of Shaw memorabilia. Violet, whose memories are quoted in the Guide Book, still finds a chair or table in the wrong place when she revisits the house. But she is delighted that the gardens and grounds have now been restored to the way they were in her day. In addition to the attractions of Shaw's Corner in its own right, some of Shaw's plays are staged in the summer months on the restored lawns.

I must say I wasn't at all sure what Mr Shaw would have thought of the proceedings. There were special events for children, and they were scampering around and making a noise. 'Living with the Shaws' was never like that! It was very different from the peace and quiet that was the rule in my day.

I have always enjoyed the links with the old days, but I never suspected that they would lead to anything more. In 2000,

Violet wearing a scarf given to her by Mrs Shaw

I heard from a lady called Christina Hardyment, a journalist and a social historian who is interested in the way households in the big houses were run in the old days. (She's written a book about it.) She informed me that some people were making a film, to be called *Gosford Park*, and they wanted to pick the brains of someone who had been in service in those days. They had asked Christina for suggestions as to who could help. When she visited Ayot, the custodians gave her my name and address.

Christina contacted me and asked to come for a visit. She wanted to pass my name on to the film people and also to do an interview herself. She wrote an article for *The Times* which covered my years at Chequers and Downing Street as well as my time with the Shaws.

Christina brought a photographer with her – Andy Swann from *The Times*. He took two different photos, one informal, where I'm sitting in my chair knitting, and another more formal one. When he came to do the second one he said, 'Would

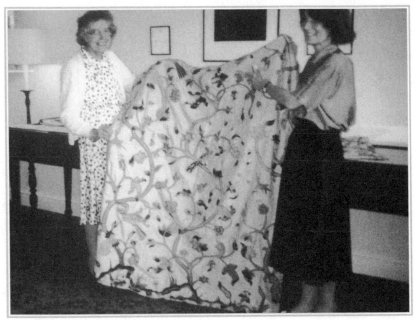

Violet and the custodian of Shaw's Corner, holding up the William Morris bedspread

you sit how you were sitting before? Because you've got very pretty legs.' Well, I'd never been told that before!

With my strict upbringing, I'd not been a cinema-goer – so the film world was a closed book to me. When I was asked to be an adviser for *Gosford Park*, it opened up a whole new world. I was to go to a flat in London, behind the Albert Hall, and meet Robert Altman, who was the director of the film, and David Levy, the producer.

ROBERT ALTMAN (B.1920)

Robert Altman was born in Kansas City, the eldest son of a wealthy businessman. From the age of twenty he began writing screenplays, and after a stint in the US Air Force, he joined the Calvin Company and began his film career by making documentary and training films for the firm. He went on to work for several TV companies, directing television series and documentaries before founding his own production company. Success came when he was offered the script for the black comedy drama *M*A*S*H**, which became a huge international success. He has directed a steady stream of films, many of them going against Hollywood conventions and methods. He has won numerous awards but some consider *Gosford Park* his best film to date.

A lady driver came to fetch me – and would you believe it, the journey from Aylesbury to London took four whole hours. That's two or three times as long as it should! I'm not sure what the hold-up was, and the driver couldn't find out. She kept getting on the phone to the office, to let them know what was happening. I knew from her anxious looks that they were saying: 'You've got an old lady in the car – is she all right?' I felt sorry for her. She kept asking me, 'Are you all right?' and I kept reassuring her.

When we finally arrived and Robert Altman and David Levy met us, peering at me to make sure they'd got the right person, my first words were, 'Could I go in there, please?' – and I made a dive for the toilet.

That afternoon was a lovely experience. They were so kind and courteous. I was in a different world, and they, for their part, could hardly imagine the world that I described to them and some of the conditions I'd taken for granted. They seemed to be amazed that there was harmony in the kitchen.

Robert Altman asked, 'Do you mean to say you didn't have quarrels and scenes?'

'No,' I assured him, 'Mrs Shaw used to say, "Eruptions in the kitchen have a terrible effect on the food."'

ARTHUR INCH

Arthur Inch was a prime adviser for the film *Gosford Park*, and it was on the set at Pinewood Studios that Violet met him. He had been trained by his father for a life in private service and worked his way up to become first footman to the Duke of Marlborough at Blenheim Palace, where there were thirty-six indoor staff alone, as well as countless gardeners and outdoor staff. Later he became under-butler to the Marquis of Londonderry in Park Lane, London. The highlight of his life was attending the coronation of King George VI in 1937, dressed in the Marquis' full state livery. 'When I was at Blenheim Palace I sometimes had the unenviable task of valeting Mr Churchill,' he commented grimly. His memories of the great man do not coincide with Violet's experiences. Arthur Inch's book *Dinner is Served* was published in 2000 and is described as 'A Butler's Guide to the Art of the Table'.

They asked all the questions, and I answered as best I knew from my experience. When it seemed time to leave I thought

I had better make the first move, so I just said, 'I know you gentlemen are too courteous to tell me to go . . .'

But before I left and the lady driver took me home, Robert Altman said, 'Give her the script,' and I was to read it and let them know of anything that seemed out of place to me.

When David Levy phoned to know if I'd read it and what I thought about it, I said, 'Yes, I do have a problem – I'd like to give it a bit of a twist, because it isn't just how it was then.'

It was hard to explain what was wrong but it didn't quite ring true to those times. The whole feel was more like things are today, there was not the respect or the discretion that there used to be among the servants.

He was lovely and so understanding, and at least I was able to give him a few examples of little things that were out of place. One thing was that the housekeeper had a clipboard – well, they weren't around then. And she wouldn't have stood for swearing. If anyone had said a wrong word, she would have dealt with it immediately and called out 'Language!'

Overall, I suppose it was the attitude of the gentry to the staff that was different from how it had been in my day. I had a cup of tea at Shepperton Studios with Arthur Inch, someone else who was advising on *Gosford Park*, and we compared notes. He had worked at one of the big houses, and he said, 'You respected them and they respected you, and there was no difficulty.'

And he was right. The gentlemen knew how to conduct themselves in all different situations. People have built up their own picture of what Mr Shaw and Mr Churchill were like, but that wasn't my experience. They were courteous and gentle towards us. I suppose that's how I found *Gosford Park* a bit off beam.

GOSFORD PARK

The setting of the film *Gosford Park* is a 1930s British country house, with its separate life above and below stairs, and the occasion is a weekend shooting party with an assortment of guests. Then a murder is committed – and must be solved. The film, directed by Robert Altman and produced by David Levy, hosts a gallery of brilliant actors, all stars in their own right. It was hugely popular on both sides of the Atlantic.

If a period piece so essentially British was to ring true, it was important to get the smallest details right. And that is why Violet's help was needed. Christina Hardyment, journalist, social historian and writer, was asked if she could suggest any people who had been 'in service' during the thirties to advise so that the film was authentic. Christina frequently visited National Trust properties for her research and told the custodian at Shaw's Corner about the request; she recommended Violet.

I had a second trip to the London flat, this time to meet the actresses. I thought they would be a bit on their dignity and perhaps showing off a bit, but none of them were like that. They greeted me as if I was a long-lost aunt! I need not have worried about what I was going to say because they kept plying me with questions. They were so keen to get it right for the film. They couldn't believe their ears when I told them what long hours we worked and how little time off we had and what we were paid. They were horrified.

Still from the film of *Gosford Park*

Then Robert Altman asked, 'What about romance?'

So I said, 'No time for it – but it would have been nice if it had happened!'

Afterwards he addressed the actresses, and they listened so hard – I thought how many church ministers would be glad of a congregation like that. They were really soaking up everything he told them. When they all trooped off, they were each given a pretty little basket, with some memento in it I think. They seemed very pleased, and you could see they were determined to do their bit to make the film a success. When I arrived home I just couldn't come down to earth again, and I had to phone Clifford and get it all off my chest. I was just full of it.

I had one more visit to make, and that was to the large house in Hertfordshire where the filming was to be done. One of the actresses, Finty Williams, who was to play the housemaid, could not be at the London meeting, and she specially wanted to make sure she got her role right. (In real life, she's Judi Dench's daughter.)

It was a beautiful house, and we were taken into the library. I expected to be asked questions as I had been before, but when she didn't speak I began talking about things myself.

'I'm afraid that fireplace is all wrong for a start,' I said and explained how the fire-irons and hearth should have been cleaned. (Some time later, on the phone, I asked David Levy what they had done about the fireplace. 'Well,' he said, 'after all you'd said we were so afraid of getting it wrong that we told the cameramen to leave it out of the picture as far as possible!')

On one occasion when Robert Altman was called to the phone, David Levy was reading a book by Christina Hardyment, I think, and he looked up and said, 'I've been reading this about the duties of the nursery maid. But when she started work she hadn't had any breakfast!'

'No,' I said, 'she wouldn't have had. She might have had a cup of tea but not breakfast. You would have a proper breakfast at the organised time – about eight o'clock – but you'd done a lot of work before then.'

I pointed out some of the books in the library that had been damaged. They were beautiful leather-bound books, but some had been sadly spoiled by the way they had been cleaned and dusted. Of course, in those days we weren't into preservation; it was just a matter of getting everything clean.

In the end I turned to Finty Williams and said, 'Now what is it you would like to know?'

Her first question was, 'How did you get the washing done?'

'I don't know any more about washing than I learned at school,' I told her, 'everything went to the laundry.'

But I did go on to tell them about Reckitt's Blue and discovered that they'd never heard of it. So next day I tried to buy one at the corner shop, and Mrs Pearce, who usually stocks everything, told me that they are no longer allowed to make them. All because of these EU regulations!

I was invited to the first night of the film, but it really wouldn't have been my scene. I would have been out of my depths. It would be a very posh affair, and I've never been into cinema-going.

Another thing, it was to be on a Sunday, and my Sundays are special. I was already committed to playing the organ as I usually do at the church service. So I asked them if Christina Hardyment could go in my place, and they were happy to arrange that.

Now, more changes have come, as I'm registered partially blind. Although I've managed pretty well on my own, I can well understand that Clifford and my niece and her husband felt that I should move near to them into sheltered accommodation, where I'd have my meals prepared. They would be near enough to visit me. At last a place was free at a Baptist Home near Ipswich. The time came to pack up my bits and pieces and leave my flat in Buckinghamshire for a new home.

When I look back on my life, I wonder at the way things have worked out. It may not have been the way I had hoped, and it may seem a bit disjointed, with lots of odd bits and pieces. But I see it more like a jigsaw, with the different bits fitting in perfectly. Every small scrap of experience has come together to prepare me for the next stage in my life. It's been a pattern not of my own but of God's making, and therefore it's been the best. I know I can trust him to fit the last few pieces, until the picture is complete and my life here on earth is done.

WHO'S WHO

Altman, Robert (b. 1925). Film director, born in Kansas City, Missouri. Served in the US Air Force. Directed *Gosford Park*, among other award-winning films.

Astor, Nancy (1879–1964). American-born British politician and the first woman MP to sit in Parliament. Famous society hostess at Cliveden, her husband's stately home.

Attlee, Clement (1883–1967). British Labour statesman. Prime Minister of the post-war Labour government of 1945.

Bevin, Ernest (1881–1951). Trade Union leader and Labour politician, minister in Churchill's wartime cabinet and foreign minister in Attlee's Labour government.

Bland, Edith (1858–1924). Better known as E. Nesbit, author of *The Railway Children* and other children's books. She was married to the Fabian journalist, Hubert Bland.

Chamberlain, Neville (1869–1940). British Prime Minister, whose appeasement policy delayed war with Germany in 1938. Churchill took over leadership in 1940.

Channon, Henry 'Chips' (1897–1958). Wealthy American, born in Chicago, who settled in England. His diaries give a racy account of British high life in the thirties.

Cherry-Garrard, Apsley (1886–1959). Young member of Scott's final expedition to the Antarctic. He later recorded his experiences in the book *The Worst Journey in the World.* In 1939, he married Angela Cherry-Garrard, née Turner (b. 1918), who was thirty years his junior. She made him supremely happy and cared for him till his death.

Churchill, Clementine née Hozier (1885–1977). Wife for fifty-seven years of Winston Churchill. Charming and formidable in her own right, she supported him and engaged in Red Cross and other war work herself.

Churchill, Sir Winston Leonard Spencer (1874–1965). English statesman, author and orator, described as 'the greatest living Englishman' especially for his leadership and victory in World War II.

Cripps, Sir Richard Stafford (1889–1952). Nephew of Beatrice Webb; chemist, lawyer and English Labour statesman who believed in applying Christianity to politics.

Eisenhower, Dwight David (1890–1969). American general and thirty-fourth US president. He brilliantly commanded the Allied D-Day invasion of the Continental mainland in 1944.

George VI (1895–1952). Became king in 1936 on the abdication of his older brother, Edward VIII. With his wife, Queen Elizabeth, he greatly helped morale in World War II.

Grey, Lady Jane (1537–1554). Descended from Henry VII and put forward as Protestant claimant to the throne on the death of Edward VI. Queen of England for nine days and later beheaded.

Grey, Mary (1545–1578). Sister of Lady Jane. Married a commoner without royal assent and was imprisoned at Chequers. Probably finally restored to royal favour.

Hardyment, Christina. Writer, journalist and historian, who first 'discovered' Violet.

Heron, Patrick (b. 1920). English painter, writer and textile designer, and son of Tom Heron, founder of Cresta Silks in Welwyn Garden City.

Hill, Kathleen. For many years Winston Churchill's private secretary, she took over the running of Chequers when Grace Lamont retired in 1945.

Hill, Octavia (1838–1912). English philanthropist and reformer, promoter of open spaces and gardens and founder of the National Trust.

Hiller, Dame Wendy (1912–2003). Leading English actress, played Saint Joan and – at Shaw's request – Eliza Doolittle in the film *Pygmalion* and Major Barbara in the 1940 film.

Hobhouse. Family of Mrs Money-Coutts, for whom Violet worked. An ancestor, Sir John Cam Hobhouse – later Baron Broughton – was a lifelong friend of the poet Byron.

Howard, Sir Ebenezer (1850–1928). English town planner and reformer and founder of the Garden City movement.

Lawrence, T. E. (Thomas Edward) (1888–1935). Known as 'Lawrence of Arabia'. Anglo-Irish soldier who fought for the Arab cause during World War I. Author of *The Seven Pillars of Wisdom.*

Maisky, Ivan (1884–1975). Came to Britain as a political refugee in 1912, returning to Russia after the Revolution. He was Soviet Ambassador to Britain from 1933–43.

Money-Coutts. Family for whom Violet worked. Was part of a long-established banking family. Sir David, whom Violet remembers as a young man, was banker to the Queen before his retirement.

Montgomery, Bernard, First Viscount Montgomery of Alamein (1887–1976). British field marshal, commanded the Eighth Army successfully and restored morale in the North African campaign in 1941.

Morris, William (1834–1896). English socialist, craftsman, painter and poet, founder of the Craft Movement. He revolutionised furniture and house decoration design.

Patch, Blanche (1879–1966). Shaw's secretary from 1920–50. Her book, *Thirty Years with GBS* was published in 1951.

Roosevelt, Franklin Delano (1882–1945). Served four terms as president of the United States. Brought about far-reaching reforms and gave forceful leadership in World War II.

Smuts, Jan Christian (1870–1950). South African statesman and Prime Minister, who gave valuable advice and help to the Allies during World War II.

Shaw, Charlotte née Payne-Townsend (1857–1943). Irish heiress. She married Bernard Shaw in 1898.

Shaw, George Bernard (1856–1950). Irish playwright, essayist, critic and staunch member of the Fabian society. His plays embody his strong moral and socialist views.

Soames, Mary née Churchill (b. 1922). Youngest child of Winston and Clementine Churchill. Skilled, prize-winning biographer of her mother in *Clementine Churchill* (1979).

Stalin, Joseph (1879–1953). Lenin's successor who created a ruthless totalitarian state in the Soviet Union, causing the deaths of millions. Still, Russia's resistance in World War II made victory possible for the Allies.

Terry, Dame Ellen (1847–1928). English leading Shakespearean actress. Friend of Bernard Shaw. In partnership with Henry Irving she dominated the UK and US stage.

Webb, Sidney, Baron Passfield (1859–1947) and Webb, Beatrice née Potter (1858–1943). English social reformers, historians and economists. He founded the Fabian Society, and together they established the London School of Economics.

Weber, Elizabeth née Money-Coutts. A teenager during Violet's time at her home. Now married to a great grandson of Dr Herman Weber, physician to Queen Victoria, brought over from Germany by Prince Albert. He liked Britain and remained here, knighted for his services to the Crown. Both son and grandson fought for the Allies during the two world wars.

Winant, John, Gilbert (1889–1947). First Chairman of the American Social Security Board and US ambassador to Britain during World War II. A sensitive and idealistic reformer.

Woolton, Frederick James, First Baron (1883–1964). English businessman and politician. Successful Minister of Food during World War II.

GLOSSARY

Abbreviations

ATS – Auxiliary Territorial Service – name given to the women's army

MP – Member of Parliament

VE Day – Victory in Europe, 8 May 1945

VJ Day – Victory in Japan, 15 August 1945

RAF – Royal Air Force

WAAF – Women's Auxiliary Air Force

Terms

Aberdonian – An inhabitant of Aberdeen, a city in northern Scotland.

Albert Hall – Opened in 1871 under Royal Charter. Situated in Kensington, London, it has provided a cultural centre for the country and is probably best known as the venue for the annual Proms (Promenade Concerts).

Amami shampoo – Popular make of shampoo advertised by the slogan 'Friday night is Amami night'.

Boanerges – Jesus' nicknamed the brothers James and John, two of his disciples, Boanerges, meaning 'sons of thunder'. T. E. Lawrence (of Arabia) gave that name to all his motorcycles.

Boiler – A closed domestic fire, burning solid fuel and used to heat water.

Brasso – A popular household cleaning fluid for brass and metal.

Celanese – A soft, silky form of rayon; a synthetic material made mainly from wood-pulp used for lingerie before the invention of nylon.

Civvie Street – Slang term for civilian life, outside the armed forces.

Claridge's Hotel – The haunt of the great and famous for over 150 years. It is still the London hotel of choice for visiting royalty and celebrities of every kind.

Clinker – Lumps of fused ash which will not burn and were therefore removed from the fire.

Coke – A solid fuel product used for firing domestic boilers.

Coster or **costermonger** – A person who sells fruit and vegetables from a barrow in town streets, particularly in London.

Coutts Bank – Long-established and highly exclusive firm of London bankers.

Demob, demobbed – Short for 'demobilisation', or being released from the services.

Doodlebugs – Popular name for 'flying bombs', or 'buzz bombs' – pilotless planes or V1s, used by the Germans against Britain in 1944.

Four-in-hand – A coach or carriage drawn by a four-horse team.

Gig – A light, two-wheeled, one-horse carriage without a hood.

Great Hall at Chequers – This hall is two stories high, with a gallery, and is the central focus of the house; it was created in the nineteenth century from an inner Elizabethan courtyard and restored in 1909.

Guinea – A British gold coin, taken out of circulation in 1813, worth twenty-one shillings. The price tag of a guinea (£1.05) continued to be used for over a hundred years.

Haberdasher – In Britain, a shop selling small articles used in sewing, such as buttons and ribbon and thread.

Libby's milk – Evaporated milk, sold in tins, sometimes used as a substitute for cream.

Lifebuoy soap – Red, carbolic soap, advertised in wartime as a freshener and deodorant.

London City Mission – Founded in 1835 to bring the Christian gospel – in word and action – to the filthy and criminal conditions of Dickensian London. Missioners were – and still are – assigned to various groups (such as, railway staff, taxi-cab drivers, actors) as well as visiting areas with special needs and providing care for the homeless.

London School of Economics – A college of London University, founded by Sidney and Beatrice Webb, originally as a centre of Fabianism, now with worldwide academic reputation.

Mansion polish – Popular furniture polish – according to 1950s advertisements, it 'makes floors shine like mirrors'.

Mennonite church – A Protestant denomination, founded in the sixteenth-century, which does not believe in infant baptism or church organisation.

Pit village – A small community of houses and shops; people living there served and depended entirely on the colliery nearby.

Range (kitchen) – A large cooking stove with burners and one or more ovens, fired usually by solid fuel.

Reckitt's Blue – Produced by Reckitt and Sons from the mid-nineteenth century. A small bag of blue dye put into the laundry to make whites look whiter.

Reserved occupation – Trade or profession of national importance during wartime (such as farming), which exempted members from call-up.

Sankey, Ira – American evangelist, hymn-writer and singer, who accompanied D. L. Moody on his missions in US and UK. His compositions formed a large part of the once-popular hymn-book *Sacred Songs and Solos*.

Scott's Emulsion – Favourite early twentieth-century home remedy to build up children's strength. Advertisements showed a fisherman holding a large fish on his back.

Shaftesbury Society – A national Christian charity providing care for people with disabilities, the elderly, unemployed and those on low income, working in partnership with churches and local authorities. The Seventh Earl of Shaftesbury (b.1801) was president of the Ragged School Union which provided free schooling and training for young people. In 1944, a hundred years later, the name was changed to the Shaftesbury Society.

Siren suit – A zip-up all-in-one suit which became Churchill's favourite wear during the war and to the end of his life. Lady Churchill designed them in various materials, including velvet for evening wear.

Times **newspaper** – The *Daily Universal Register*, established in 1785, became *The Times* in 1788. Once a newspaper of influence and reliability, it has now become much like other popular broadsheets.

Trooping the Colour – Annual ceremony in which a regimental colour (or flag) is paraded before the monarch.

Wesleyan chapel – 'Preaching houses' or Wesleyan chapels set up following the preaching mission of John and Charles Wesley which began in 1739. By 1830 there was one in most towns and villages. In 1932 Wesleyan, Primitive Methodists and United Methodists joined together, but the amalgamation took some time to come into effect locally.

Zebo – Cleaning material for cast iron grates requiring plenty of elbow polish to give the required shine.

We want to hear from you. Please send your comments about this book to us in care of zreview@zondervan.com. Thank you.

GRAND RAPIDS, MICHIGAN 49530 USA

WWW.ZONDERVAN.COM